Systemic Supervision

A Portable Guide for Supervision Training

*Gill Gorell Barnes, Gwynneth Down
and Damian McCann*

with contributions by Nuala Sheehan and Paul Blackburn

Jessica Kingsley Publishers
London and Philadelphia

First published in the United Kingdom in 2000 by
Jessica Kingsley Publishers Ltd
116 Pentonville Road
London N1 9JB, England
and
325 Chestnut Street,
Philadelphia, PA19106, USA

www.jkp.com

Copyright ©2000 Gill Gorell Barnes, Gwynneth Down and Damian McCann
Copyright ©2000 Chapter Two Nuala Sheehan
Copyright ©2000 Chapter Three Paul Blackburn

Library of Congress Cataloging in Publication Data
Barnes, Gill Gorell.
    Systemic supervision: a portable model for supervision training / Gill Gorell Barnes, Gwynneth Down and Damian McCann
        p. cm.
    Includes bibliographical references and index.
    ISBN 1-85302-853-3 (pbk. : alk. paper)
    1. Social workers--Supervision of. 2. Social workers--Training of. I. Down, Gwynneth, 1960- II. McCann, Damian.
    HV40.54.B37 2000
    361.13'069'3--dc21   99-056653

British Library Cataloguing in Publication Data
A CIP catalogue record for this book is available from the British Library

ISBN 1 85302 853 3 pb

Printed and Bound in Great Britain by
Athenaeum Press, Gateshead, Tyne and Wear

Contents

Foreword

This book addresses supervision and the development of supervision within agency contexts in the current field of family therapy in the UK. The formal links between practice in different settings (social service, mental health, hospitals, child and adult psychiatry), the regulating structures that have developed over the last decade and the theories that contextualise systemic supervision and systemic practice have posed new areas of interest and concern for trainers who are developing standards within the field. The book originated in a pioneer course, 'Training for Supervision', developed through the Institute of Family Therapy with Gill Gorell Barnes as supervisor. We would like to thank the other people who helped make that course possible and who made sure that it was completed, particularly Gwyn Daniel, Sarah Barratt and Judy Hildebrand, all of whom consulted to us and acted as assessors. Their comments in turn provoked new trajectories in course development and with developments in the life of the course. Other colleagues who were part of the original team included Nancy Graham, Peter Bishop and Judith Lask. Each of them contributed to the life and thinking of the course and to the range of theory and practice that was available. We would also like to thank the trainee family therapists who participated in the agency team contexts; they provided the stimulus of their own learning to the supervisor's development. In particular we would like to thank Annette Allen and Lorraine Davis, who have contributed their thoughts to a chapter on the trainee's perspective. We would also like to thank Judith Lask for her contribution, and Margaret Bennett who co-authored 'Points to consider when establishing clinical placements for trainee family therapists' (Appendix III), and for helping to obtain permission to use *The Red Book* (the AFT guidelines for supervisory training).

Lastly, we would like to thank the Institute of Family Therapy (London) who, as a hosting organisation, provided much of the unseen help and support that is often not named. Our thanks in particular go to Gillian Russell who helped us redraft the guidelines and the revised accreditation requirements on many occasions.

The guidelines for the supervisor's course we established were in parallel to the guidelines being drawn up by the Association of Family Therapy, which have since superseded them as good practice requirements. The course was marked by an emphasis on co-construction of ideologies about supervision – ideas about what was required at different levels of good practice and areas of knowledge that trainee supervisors thought it would be essential for a supervisor to cover. The course included peer group supervision as well as agency-based supervision training. The latter was contextualised by the need for a clearer hierarchical distinction between a supervisor, who would be clinically responsible for all the cases seen, and trainees seeing the families, who would come from a range of disciplines and have different years of experience in the field. On-site visits were made by the course supervisor to each of the qualifying trainees on several occasions. This was not only to build up the number of hours of supervised practice, but also to understand some of the particular issues that accompany running training teams in agency contexts.

The book aims to provide a companion guide and thoughtful reader for anyone who is attempting supervision or who is themselves in the process of being supervised. *Chapter 1* covers the current context of family therapy in the UK – its formal links and structures, and the theories that contextualise systemic supervision and systemic practice, including attention to belief systems and shared social constructions at different levels of the supervision team. The therapist's own life experience as it resonates with constantly changing constructions of family life, and the way this has led to a more reflexive approach to supervision, is contrasted with earlier UK writing about supervision, and changes over the last two decades are discussed. The chapter introduces current requirements for supervision training, and ways of addressing these are covered in greater detail in the chapters that follow. In *Chapter 2* we discuss the creation and running of a structure for developing a higher level of training within a mental health trust, working simultaneously at clinical and academic levels. The work involved included outreach work to agencies in the community and the holding of responsibility for case management to line managers. The structure of the team and ways of handling potentially incongruous professional and gender hier-archies are discussed. *Chapter 3* discusses 'fit' at different levels of the context of therapy training. To what extent is the agency in which the trainer works ready to become a context for formal professional development? How ready is the training therapist when it comes to exploring aspects of his/her self, as provoked by different client families? How can 'family of origin' work for the therapist be appropriately built into a training team where people also work together in other contexts? How can therapists and supervisors formulate ways of addressing their own ignorance about aspects of family life that clients have more knowledge of than they do themselves? *Chapter 4* is written from the point of view of a supervisor struggling to define the nature of the supervisory relationship within a training context, and offers a developmental framework. The tensions inherent in supervising trainees at different levels of professional and clinical development are addressed. The choice of a theoretical framework for 'live' supervision, and the movement in the supervisor's mind between creating safe structures for learning and developing a practice that values uncertainty and multiple perspectives, is explored in the context of an on-site training team. *Chapter 5* explores the views of trainees themselves on their supervised clinical training. Issues discussed include the settings and their formal position within it, the setting and the training teams working out responsibility for learning, contracts with the training setting, addressing issues of power and difference, and the experiences of working in the training team, as well as the effects of different methods of supervision.

The next three chapters address key dimensions of self that contextualise all systemic practice and, therefore, supervision training. These are culture, gender and sexuality. *Chapter 6* addresses the fit between theory, practice and cultural complexity. A model of attending to institutional racism within all levels of the family team and supervision hierarchy is described. Creating a context for multicultural thinking within both training and treatment contexts is outlined with an emphasis on deconstructing stereotypical thinking and re-acculturating the mind of the therapist. *Chapter 7* considers some of the issues that men and women have faced over the last twenty years in defining their differences from one another and what they have in common in relation to therapeutic ideals. Giving a brief history of the impact of feminist thinking on the early family therapy training in this country, the chapter emphasises how for different theoretical orientations, the deconstruction of gender and gender premises can be central to freeing men and women from outdated or oppressive premises, giving space for creative thinking. *Chapter 8* focuses on issues of the sexual self as this is brought into, or withheld from, the arena of therapeutic practice and training. As one of the many conversations about the self in therapy, sexuality is often marginalised or disqualified altogether. This chapter addresses some of the preliminary conversations that might begin within teams in order to make the field more open to including sexuality among the other many conversations it has embraced. Case examples relating to different sexualities, and exercises addressing dilemmas that may arise for therapists, are given.

Throughout the book a range of clinical examples are used to connect the questions under discussion to clinical practice. In some sections of the book exercises are offered that may help develop greater fluency in thinking about difficult topics. Throughout the book we have taken a 'more questions than answers' approach to topics that we are addressing, but have nonetheless tried to make clear areas that we feel it is essential to include in the supervisory mind and arena of training.

Gill Gorell Barnes

1

Into the Millennium

Gill Gorell Barnes and Damian McCann

The history of family systems theory and practice has seen many exciting developments over time. Once described as a major epistemological revolution (Sluzki 1978), family systemic therapy and its proponents currently appear to be in the process of consolidation. To some extent this may be viewed as a sign of maturity, but it is also consistent with developments generally within the field – in terms of establishing standards of professional practice and protecting credibility. For example, ethical guidelines, which have always existed, have now been formalised and enshrined in codes of conduct. Registering bodies now oversee the work of others, and new systems have emerged to administer and regulate what was once a wide open space. Although this may, to some extent, have had a stultifying effect on those wishing to deliver new brush strokes, the current preoccupation of attending to the detail within these larger frames has done much to ensure the continued development, and indeed growth, of family and systemic practice as we enter the new millennium.

The formalisation of the training of family and systemic practitioners has now reached the supervisory domain. This is reflected in the sudden increase in courses relating to supervision, which offer practitioners the opportunity of becoming qualified supervisors. Already, the Association for Family and Systemic Practice have produced *The Red Book*, which outlines the requirements for the registration of supervisors and the accreditation of training courses (Association for Family Therapy 1996). A similar but much more substantial text was produced by The American Association for Marriage and Family Therapy (AAMFT) in October 1997. Entitled *AAMFT Approved Supervisors...Mentors and Teachers for the Next Generation of MFTs: Approved Supervisor Designation Standards and Responsibilities Handbook*, prospective supervisors are left in no doubt that the journey towards attaining approved status is indeed a serious business.

Both handbooks spell out in some detail the various component parts and the requisite number of supervised hours that are required. For instance, AAMFT insist that supervisors-in-training must meet the educational, experiential and supervisory requirements (incorporating a number of learning objectives, as well as a set number of supervised hours) which must then be successfully integrated into a coherent theory and practice of marriage and family therapy supervision. AFT (the Association for Family Therapy), similarly, requires applicants to demonstrate reflexive competence in the areas of practice, theory, personal development and ethics. Each of these aspects are broken down into sections and the requirements relating to each area of competence are carefully outlined. For instance, with regard to practice, the Association for Family Therapy and Systemic Practice criteria for approved supervision training, *The Red Book*, suggests that the supervisors-in-training must have the ability to 'use a range of supervisory techniques in the supervision of systemic family therapists' (page 4). And in the area of personal development, he/she must have the ability to 'recognise and understand patterns from within their own significant relationships systems (past, present and future)' (page 5). (For further information concerning the specific requirements as outlined by the Association for Family Therapy and Systemic Practice, the reader is referred to Appendix I.)

In this book we present some of the issues involved in creating and attaining settings for learning and training, and for meeting the contextual requirements for achieving supervisory status. We describe models of supervision that have been tried and tested in different National Health Service settings, and that have become part of established local training resources. By naming it 'portable supervision', we are outlining some of the ways in which therapists who want to develop family therapy training settings in their own areas (which will involve them in supervising family therapy in action) can set up training units within their own work settings. Once the territory is defined they can address the necessary range of issues that will qualify them as supervisors of systemic therapists.

How to position this book

This book evolved from a course that was originally designed to meet the AFT requirements for qualification as a systemic supervisor, which were co-evolving with other requirements from regulatory bodies. Externally, the reference points included the European Association for Psychotherapy, the United Kingdom Council for Psychotherapy, and the National Health Service review of psychotherapy services. From these different perspectives issues such as the number of hours required to achieve a qualification in supervision vied uneasily with what those hours would contain; and tensions existed around how a common purpose in the training of psychotherapists could co-exist with the valued discrete skills inherent within different models. The phrase 'evidence-based health care' recurred across a number of documents (Parry 1996; Roth and Fonagy 1996). In the pilot course which gave the initial impetus for this book, all course participants were practising within child and family or adult mental health services where supervision was felt to be an urgent need. Many of the larger issues defining therapy and evidence-based practice, and the relationship of these to supervision, formed a key part of course discussion and development.

Theories that contextualise systemic supervision

A systemic approach to work with individuals, couples and families can be distinguished from other therapeutic orientations and their models for supervision in a number of ways. First, it looks at current context, in terms of what is going on in people's lives now, as well as what has gone on in the past. Second, it listens to the ways in which current relationships, as well as former relationships, come to form patterns and conversations in people's minds, and therefore influence their beliefs and daily practices. The practice base from which this awareness is developed comes from watching and listening to people describing their lives and dilemmas within the context of their own living relationships, with all the editing and hesitations this inevitably produces. Third, the way in which these inner and outer conversations are arranged – what is said and not said, the importance different individuals accord to different nuances of the same description, and the way some are privileged over others – is seen by family therapists as related to the ways in which entanglements, misunderstandings and conflicts can arise and be perpetuated over time. These interactions may be acted out in intimate relationships, in extended families and in wider interpersonal contexts.

Supervision of systemic practice therefore requires attention to the different subsystems that evolve within the current context of therapy, the therapeutic system formed by therapist and family and the changes that take place in this context over time. The different levels of understanding and connection between all who form the therapeutic system, and the way in which the whole is developing, require attentive and open listening. An explicit attention to the layers of social construction in the 'thing that is being observed' has now become a more familiar part of supervisor and team process and will be developed further in the book. Supervision requires a wide-angle lens, an accurately focused zoom facility and the ability to receive and process multiple communications, some of which may be in conflict.

Systemic practice

A number of different activities in relation to ideas of mind and context are included in systemic practice:

- philosophies of how to observe and frame relational events
- methods of description that explicitly make connections between people and their wider social context

- relational approaches to treating dilemmas and problems in families and human systems
- a number of therapeutic methods addressing these, with particular skills devolving from each approach.

Since within the modality systemic therapy considers problems in the larger context of the wider social and political structures of which the family and the therapist are each an evolving part, ways of addressing this commonality have increasingly entered the field. This has also created new ways of considering the supervisory process as one that includes many layers of mutual influence or 'reflexivity'.

Meanings and beliefs

In developing a training model for supervision in systemic family therapy, a number of levels that make up the worlds of family, therapist and supervisor have to be taken into account.

Individual beliefs and family beliefs

These include the development of individual beliefs and ways of construing the world; the way individual beliefs are constrained by family beliefs and family patterns; the way families communicate with one another and how that affects the individuals within them and their freedom to think, act and speak; the nuances of family languages and their specific context-determined meanings, and the way these relate to the development of individual meanings and individual narrative. Each of these will play a part in how the therapist reads the family, how the family read the therapist and the way the supervisor manages (or does not) to keep a mind that is open to the possible variations of meaning and understanding exchanged before them in the room. A further component will be the therapist's own process of assigning meaning and emphasis to what they are seeing, hearing and experiencing.

What are we supervising? Client(s) and therapist

- the presenting problem and the relationship pattern. Where is the 'fit' between therapist and family?
- current context – interactions, behaviours and conversations
- patterns in the mind: beliefs and inner monologues
- hierarchy of discourses, both outer and inner
- former patterns and their influence on current patterns (both intergenerational and within a current life).

Socially constructed beliefs

At a higher level of social patterning the way family, therapist and supervisors are themselves constrained by gender, culture, ethnicity or class will play an ongoing part in any clinical training group. The descriptions of family life generated from these different positions will operate with different effects in the self-descriptions of any member of family or team. Common assumptions based on social descriptions such as 'lone parent', 'divorced father' or 'foreigner' may therefore form part of the intersubjective language and understanding of the supervised therapy. Ideas about the 'self' and the connections between subjective descriptions and ideas that are socially constructed and sometimes pathologised, emerging from the accounts of others, are an integral part of what emerges in the discourses created within the context of therapy. These often reverberate from client to therapist or to supervisor, or to all levels in a supervisory system. Tuning into these reverberations appropriately requires constant vigilance and thoughtfulness on the supervisor's part. The movement backwards and forwards between clients' voices, personal experience for therapist and/or supervisor, and that which can be learned from research and theory, itself characterised the development of our own supervision training. This 'circular' movement encouraged us to construct a range of ways of viewing families, therapist and supervisor as subject to similarly socially constructed principles. Including discussions about gender, role and culturally determined expectations of men and women, boys and girls, and their behaviours, as some of the many strands in conversations between supervisor and therapists, provoked fresh thinking for each of us.

Shared social constructions: The worlds of client, therapist and supervisor

Working with colleagues of different ethnicities, as well as with families from across the world, further increased our sensitivity to the plurality of experience (Gorell Barnes 1998; Thomas 1995). Working with gay and lesbian couples, both with their families of origin and as couples on their own (which subsequently developed into a specialist service offered by the Institute of Family Therapy (McCann and Graham 1997)), further encouraged the deconstruction of any 'totalising' approach to the idea of 'family' itself, and moved us further in the direction of considering the 'hierarchy of discourses' within a therapy session.

We analysed the voices at different levels of social patterning as follows:

- gender and expected gender role in immediate, extended and intergenerational family
- class and expected 'role' behaviour – compliant and non-compliant
- religion and its dictates about moral/ethical behaviour
- culture and its dictates about moral/ethical/nurturant behaviour

- ethnicity and the imperatives embedded in the expectations of elders, survivors and other loved ones as above

- sexuality and group loyalties to current constructions of appropriate behaviour within the group; gay, lesbian, hetero or bisexual.

Giving attention to which of these discourses was privileged over others, and the way in which some discourses and stories about family life and family functioning predominate, came to be a regular part of our approach to the work, both with clients and therapist.

Further voices at different levels of social patterning were:

- Importance for the therapist of holding all the family in mind and enquiring how members not present are held in the minds of those who are.

- Many people, whether past, absent or present, make up 'voices in the mind' or components of self.

- Voices may come from many differing contexts, some of which may compete with one another.

- Voices of gender, class, ethnicity, religion and culture, which include the expectations of extended families in the UK or other countries, may all bring different perspectives to bear on current individual and family discourses.

The therapist's own life experience and self-development

In helping a therapist to be attuned to how a family's history may affect their current thinking about a problem or a life dilemma, most supervisors will encourage them to look at their own life situation, using methods that are similar to those they might employ with a family in therapy. The experience of connection between one thing and another is then held at a personal as well as a theoretical level, a 'lived experience' as well as an observed experience (Reiss 1989). While it is a common experience that this is part of training in relation to earlier parts of a therapist's life story, it is less common to examine reflexivities in the therapist's current life context (see 'Personal development' on page 22). Issues of boundary between the personal and the professional self are of particular importance where colleagues also work with each other outside the supervision setting, so that the team cannot function as a 'safe' boundaried place in the same way that a stranger group, meeting only for the purposes of clinical work and supervision, might. (Questions raised by working as a supervisor in a shared work setting are discussed throughout, particularly in Chapters 2 and 3).

Transitions, losses and family life

The increase in transition as part of many families' experience – transitions created by separations through migration, death, divorce and family re-ordering of many kinds – require a therapist to be attuned both to losses and to how continuities of belief may continue in spite of the changes in relationships and shifts in the structures of family life. This may be as true among professionals seeing families as it is among families currently seeking therapeutic help, and relates both to common experiences of migration and to the common experiences of transitions following divorce and, more rarely, death. As more families separate and new partnerships are formed, it is likely that the experience of continuous and discontinuous relationships, and the dilemmas and 'mind muddles' that may go alongside such transitions, will be a part of the therapeutic system at one or more levels – supervisor, therapist or family.

Changing therapeutic constructions of family life

Early family therapy training (as described in a brief review of Whiffen and Byng-Hall, 1982, page 19) was based on a theory of the family as a stable, two-parent social system that remained together over time. However, constructions of family life have changed over the last two decades. A number of influences have contributed to new thinking. First, the structures of family life in the UK have themselves diversified. Changes in patterns of cohabitation, childbearing and marriage are each different to a generation ago with women cohabiting, and up to one-third having babies, before they marry. While this should have led to many changes in thinking about family life, such normative experiences are still sometimes described in pejorative ways. There are also many varieties of transitional life experience that a therapist will need to take into account, and these are constantly evolving. Lone parenthood, serial cohabitation and step-families are three forms of family life involving many normal transitional experiences which are often insufficiently understood by therapists or supervisors, as are the varied discourses of adoption, artificial insemination by donor and the increasing number of changing birth technologies which bring their own risks and resiliencies. The notion of stability and continuity in family life which used to be seen as forming part of a well-regulated society and functionally organised at different and complementary levels has opened to new fluctuations and uncertainties. It was around notions of unitary coherence in family structure and function that early systems thinking was developed (Jackson 1957, 1965), but thinking about what therapy with families involves has undergone many changes which themselves carry implications for the supervisory process.

Rethinking family bonds: Diversity, intimacy and identity

The diversity of race and culture within UK society has now led to therapists' awareness of their own ignorance about the many functional structures for bringing up children and greater curiosity about what is unfamiliar. This has contributed to supervisors often taking a position of 'not knowing' rather than 'knowing more', which can itself bring about confusion in the supervisory process (see Chapter 4). Diversity within teams and a willingness to exchange and examine difference in experience has replaced a model of the one-way exchange of information, 'from the top down', and led to more comfort with the reflexivities between lives on each side of a screen (see Chapters 6 and 8).

It has also led to the search for clearer knowledges about how 'family' works on behalf of its different members, including the young and the old. In Western societies, theorising about the family has often privileged the central importance of the husband–wife bond, taking as desirable 'norms' equality between partners, empathy for one another's experience and a willingness to collaborate around both meaning and action (Gorell Barnes 1994; Rampage 1994). The importance of connectedness in other relationships such as mother–son, father–brother, sister–brother or mother–child that give meanings to the idea of 'family' have been marginalised in Western theorising about family, and therefore also in theories informing family therapy. Psychotherapy has only recently begun to follow wisdom from sociology, anthropology or writings from cultures other than Northern European–based, that draws attention to the significance of intimacies within larger kinship groups for secure family identity as well as for secure gendered identity. Beliefs qualifying the limits of intimate relationships of different kinds, and the effects of these beliefs on different behaviours in families, what is permitted in the way of open talk within different sections of a family and what is forbidden, distorted or concealed, have different impacts on freedom to think within the diversity of the family. Therapists and supervisors therefore need to develop appropriate curiosity about how to enquire into what may or may not be openly talked about (Gorell Barnes 1996, 1998).

Family therapy teaching and research, therefore, has moved towards considering diversity of process in family life, and away from ideas of family 'normality' and 'pathology'. Assumptions based on the stability of family life and the internal coherence of systems patterned over time (which developed in the 1950s and 1960s) have to be reconsidered in the light of the transitions and disruptions experienced by many families seen in clinical settings in the 1990s. The theoretical focus on patterns and rules seen to be maintaining symptoms over time which it was the therapist's job to 'discover' has changed to a more humble professional curiosity in which therapist and family consider together the changing field of life relationships and intimate experience. Certainties about family 'dysfunction' have moved towards questions about family 'function' considered through significantly different lenses of gender and culture. This has a range of implications for how supervisors might think about the supervisory process.

In the section that follows we refer to some earlier supervision writing which has had an indirect influence on our own thinking; that is, it reflects the earlier training of one of us (Gorell Barnes) who herself was the supervisor in the training team from which this book originated. We have limited ourselves to the patterns of influence recognisable in relation to the current thinking in this book.

Family therapy supervision in the UK: Earlier theory

The most comprehensive compendium of ideas on supervision in the UK, *Family Therapy Supervision*, was edited by Whiffen and Byng-Hall (1982). This contained supervision ideas written by a diverse number of authors covering some classic components of supervision techniques such as the 'genogram' that is triggered by aspects of a particular family, the 'trigger family' (McGoldrick 1982); the use of 'videotape' for retrospective supervision (Whiffen 1982); and different forms of 'live intervention' such as the 'earphone' (Byng-Hall 1982) or direct supervision in the room (Gorell Barnes and Campbell 1982; Pegg and Manocchio 1982). In the current context of supervisory development described in this book, all these techniques, aside from 'live supervision in the room' are now a 'standard' part of the repertoire of a supervisor in training. However, in reviewing aspects of these basic techniques with current supervisors in training at the Institute of Family Therapy (through the medium of a contemporary video *Closing the Gap* (1982)), current trainees took a number of different positions in relation to assumptions about power and expertise seen as implicitly embedded in many of the techniques shown on the tape. A discussion about socially constructed changes in our society as a whole, as these relate to the use of privilege and power in therapy and the way a therapist or supervisor conducts their work, was juxtaposed with the assumptions about both intervention and 'professionalism' observed on the tape. This showed how the move towards more 'open' or 'transparent' supervision has permeated the assumptive base of current supervisory thinking (see also Chapter 2, page 29). Early precursors of current openness to mutual influences in therapeutic and supervisory processes ('transparency') can be found in *Family Therapy Supervision*. These chapters lend themselves to a second reading from our current context two decades later. They include one on the use of the family's relationship to the supervision group as a therapeutic tool (Lindsey and Lloyd 1982) and one on multilevel training and supervision in an outpatient service programme (Tomm and Wright 1982). Each of these chapters illustrates aspects of the 'second order' approach, subsequently to become of such central importance in systemic thinking.

The therapist as part of the pattern: An extension of 'mutual influence'

The study of what came to be known as 'second order cybernetics', in which the role of the therapist, the therapist's meaning system and to greater or lesser degrees the supervisor's meaning system, is considered as part of the 'field' of therapeutically generated meanings, which has preoccupied family therapy theorists and supervisors since the 1980s, following developments from the 'Milan' school of family therapy (Boscolo and Cecchin 1982; Jones 1993; Campbell *et al.* 1991). The 'puzzle' posed by questions around therapist 'objectivity' and 'approximation' in relation to the assessment and measurement of 'reality' was voiced but rarely explored as part of early family systems thinking as developed by Bateson and the MRI group (Bateson 1973). The famous dictum of Korzybski (1958) – 'the map is not the territory' – was one small part of this. Subsequently, a reaction to the idea of 'objective' descriptions of family pattern (see Colapinto 1991), to the idea of 'neutrality' in the therapist's relationship with his task (Selvini Palazzolli *et al.* 1980) and to models of intervention operating as though the process of influence only went in one direction, brought the systemic therapy field as a whole back to preoccupations about the way in which the therapist in turn was influenced: observers were moved to consider 'construction' rather than 'instruction' to be the key to therapeutic work. While many workers originally trained in a psychodynamic approach argued at the time that such awareness had formerly been familiar to them under other terminology such as transference, counter-transference, projection and projective identification (Bentovim and Kinston 1991; Box 1981; Dicks 1967), psychoanalytically based assumptions failed to take account of the vital 'paradigm shifts' brought about by including social construction as an element in the theory of all therapeutic process building, *and therefore as a vital part of the supervisory process itself.* Social construction includes a recognition that people understand the world the way they do because each of us participates in wider social practices, which give shared meanings to events within relationships. As this is equally true for each of us, so it necessarily requires the deconstruction of what may be contributed by 'common' assumptions or assumptive bases for all concerned in a therapeutic enterprise. The 'unpacking' of differences in meanings, in order for shared intersubjective meanings or common assumptive bases to develop in therapy, is often a vital part of the successful therapeutic process as well as of the process of developing common languages for supervision and for supervising teams.

How is this work to be done? Achieving current requirements

In the current requirements for training set out by the Association of Family Therapy, supervisors are required to demonstrate reflexive competence in the areas of practice, personal development, ethics and theory. Theory is addressed in the chapters that follow whereas specific paragraphs on practice, personal development and ethics are contained in the next section.

The practice of supervision training

Supervised hours, which form the backbone of the training process, must be undertaken in a context that is geared for training and where the trainee practitioners are in the advanced stages of their family and systemic training. Supervisors-in-training are only authorised to supervise trainees as long as they receive ongoing supervision by an approved supervisor. The notion of 'supervised hours' incorporates both direct and indirect supervision. For instance, supervisors-in-training must be willing to have their development and skills in the practice of supervision scrutinised by an approved supervisor. This can be achieved by a mixture of live supervision (video and audio recordings) and indirect supervision (which would take the form of discussions of particular supervisory dilemmas, role play, etc.). The supervisor is ultimately responsible for the overall development of the supervisor-in-training and must be satisfied that he/she has fulfilled all the criteria laid down by the registering body.

Routes to becoming an approved supervisor are also being considered. A basic requirement for any training in the supervision of family and systemic practice is that the applicant must be a qualified or approved practitioner who has also had a period of consolidation. Qualified or approved supervisors are those who have successfully completed a recognised training in supervision or, by virtue of the longevity of experience as a supervisor, are eligible to supervise others (referred to as the grandparental scheme). (As with newly qualified practitioners, who are required to undertake further consultative hours before being eligible for registration, qualified supervisors are also required to complete a set number of hours of supervised practice before being able to supervise supervisors-in-training. The training of supervisors, or supervision-of-supervision, is currently in the process of development. At present, the AAMFT distinguishes qualified and approved practitioners in terms of task and level of training. Qualified supervisors, for instance, are those who are qualified to supervise trainee family and systemic therapists. Approved supervisors are those who are both qualified and have completed the required supervised hours to undertake higher level training – namely, supervision-of-supervision.)

At present, the accreditation and development of the supervisory domain rests with a number of institutions. Essentially, the United Kingdom Council for Psychotherapy (UKCP), through its relevant section (Family, Marital and Systemic Therapies), is responsible for the accreditation of courses leading to the qualification of family and systemic therapists, as well as those relating to the qualification of family and systemic supervisors. Both the Association for Family and Systemic Therapies and 'Confetti'[1] (through the CRED Committee), link with the UKCP in accrediting and developing courses. This obviously includes developments relating to supervisory courses and also links to ongoing discussions concerning European standards. (For a more detailed outline of the current structure, the reader is referred to Appendix II.)

The ethics of supervising training

A further area for consideration concerns that of ethics. The UKCP has developed a code of ethics to which all supervisors must subscribe. These offer standards against which potential violations provoke either formal or informal discipline. Those practising within an ethical framework would be concerned with fairness, decency and consideration of every family member's needs as well as the needs of the supervisor-in-training – loyalty, equality, reciprocity, accountability, trust, etc. There is a requirement that the ethical guidelines that operate within the training setting are clear to all concerned. Supervisors must establish ground rules that reflect ethical practice and he/she must be willing to reinforce these if, for any reason, they are breached. Clients must know who is ultimately in charge of the therapy, and there must be a clarity of roles and responsibilities with regard to the trainee and the supervisor in relation to the therapeutic work being undertaken. Ethical dilemmas must be discussed on a regular basis within the context of training, the purpose being that trainees will become empowered over time to deal with ethical issues as they arise in the work.

Personal development

The UKCP and the European Certificate for Psychotherapy have each made it a requirement for qualified practitioners in all forms of psychotherapy to have done several hundred hours of 'personal work' as part of their qualifying training. Family therapy and systemic training have not thought it appropriate for therapists to do this work within the context of their own family, and have never made it part of the training experience to 'bring their own family in'. Nonetheless, many ways of working on family experience, such as using genograms and, in earlier days, using family sculpting, have been a part of people's training experience.

One of the missing ingredients within psychotherapy training as a whole is any agreement on what 'the use of self' involves. From a systemic perspective,

---

1   Confetti is the Confederation of Family Therapy Training Institutes.

how 'self' is to be defined within a framework that often argues for a multiplicity of contextually defined selves rather than a 'core' self has sometimes led to uncertainty about how the issue of self-awareness and the physical and emotional use of self is to be developed as part of the therapist's repertoire. A recent book, *Bridging the Gap* (Hildebrand 1998), offers a range of ways in which systemic training courses can develop the appropriate complexity or match the variety of personal encounters working with families is likely to encompass. Taking as the starting point the need to devise ways of looking at the self which reflect some of the immediacy and complexity of family therapy (in which experience and change take place at a number of levels simultaneously), she describes tasks which promote greater self-reflexivity, leading to an increase in perception of the complexity of change and which make a difference to practice competence. Work takes place in a group arena, within the contexts defined by the training course. Trainees are therefore encouraged to voice aspects of their personal experience openly in ways that parallel the experience they will be asking of family members. Action, reflection and narrative about personal experience form part of the learning about the 'self in context'. In working with others while working on the self, trainees are offered an experience of shared emotional and cognitive change which characterises much of what may take place in a family session.

Further work on the self will inevitably continue throughout a therapist's working life and is a practical approach to 'supervision in context'. *Staff Supervision in a Turbulent Environment* (Hughes and Pengelly 1997) highlights ways in which such learning can continue, using the self-learning promoted by key pieces of work, the sharing of developmental life events and the impact of unexpected stressful life experience. These can all bring about leaps in a therapist's self-knowledge. In addition, crises in the workplace, natural life cycles, losses or national disasters involving colleagues may bring forth deep and empathic identifications which promote new awareness of self or consolidates former learning.

References

American Association for Marriage and Family Therapy (AAMFT) (1997) *Approved Supervisors…Mentors and Teachers for the Next Generation of MFTs: Approved Supervisor Deignation Standards and Responsibilities Handbook.* Washington DC: AAMFT Publishing.

Association for Family and Systemic Practice (1996) *The Red Book: Registration of Supervisors and Accreditation of Training Courses: Criteria and Guidelines.* London: AFT Publishing.

Bateson, G. (1973) *Steps to an Ecology of Mind.* London: Paladin.

Bentovim, A. and Kinston, W. (1991) 'Joining systems theory with psychodynamic understanding.' In A. Gurman and D.P. Kniskern (eds) *Handbook of Family Therapy* 2. New York: Brunner Mazel.

Boscolo, L. and Cecchin, G. (1982) 'Training in systemic therapy at the Milan Centre.' In R. Whiffen and J. Byng-Hall (eds) *Family Therapy Supervision: Recent Developments in Practice.* London, Toronto and Sydney: Academic Press. New York and San Francisco: Grune and Stratton.

Box, S. (1981) *Psychotherapy with Families: An Analytic Approach.* London: Routledge and Kegan Paul.

Byng-Hall, J. (1982) 'The use of the earphone in supervision.' In R. Whiffen and J. Byng-Hall (eds) *Family Therapy Supervision: Recent Developments in Practice.* London, Toronto and Sydney: Academic Press. New York and San Francisco: Grune and Stratton.

Campbell, D., Draper, R. and Crutchley, E. (1991) 'The Milan systemic approach to family therapy.' In A.S. Gurman and D.P. Kniskern (eds) *Handbook of Family Therapy*, vol.11. New York: Brunner Mazel.

Colapinto, J. (1991) 'Structural family therapy.' In A.S. Gurman and D.P. Kniskern (eds) *Handbook of Family Therapy 2.* New York: Brunner Mazel.

Dicks, H.V. (1967) *Marital Tensions: Clinical Studies towards a Psychological Theory of Interaction.* London: Routledge and Kegan Paul.

Gorell Barnes, G. (1994) 'Commentary on "Power gender and marital intimacy".' *Journal of Family Therapy 16*, 1, 139–143.

Gorell Barnes, G. (1996) 'Gender issues.' In R. Davis, G. Upton and V. Varma (eds) *The Voice of the Child.* London: Routledge.

Gorell Barnes, G. (1998) *Family Therapy in Changing Times.* Basingstoke: Macmillan.

Gorell Barnes, G. and Campbell, D. (1982) 'The impact of structural and strategic approaches on the supervision process: A supervisor is supervised, or how to progress from frog to prince: Two theories of change 1978–1980.' In R. Whiffen and J. Byng-Hall (eds) *Family Therapy Supervision: Recent Developments in Practice.* London, Toronto and Sydney: Academic Press. New York and San Francisco: Grune and Stratton.

Hildebrand, J. (1995) 'Learning through supervision: A systemic approach.' In M. Yelloly and M. Henkel (eds) *Learning and Teaching in Social Work Practice.* London: Jessica Kingsley Publishers (1998).

Hildebrand, J. (1998) *Bridging the Gap: A Training Module in Personal and Professional Development.* London: Karnac Books.

Hughes, L. and Pengelly, P. (1997) *Staff Supervision in a Turbulent Environment: Managing Process and Task in Front-Line Services.* London: Jessica Kingsley Publishers.

Jackson, D.D. (1957) 'The question of family homeostasis.' *Psychiatric Quarterly Supplement 31*, 79–90.

Jackson, D.D. (1965) 'The study of the family.' *Family Process 4*, 1–20.

Jones, E. (1993) *Family Systems Therapy: Developments in the Milan Systemic Therapies.* Chichester: John Wiley and Sons.

Korzybski, A. (1958) *Science and Saints.* Connecticut, USA: The International Non-Aristotelian Library.

Lindsey, C. and Lloyd, J. (1982) 'The use of the family's relationship to the supervision group as a therapeutic tool.' In R. Whiffen and J. Byng-Hall (eds) *Family Therapy Supervision: Recent Developments in Practice.* London, Toronto and Sydney: Academic Press. New York and San Francisco: Grune and Stratton.

McCann, D. and Graham, M. (1997) *Gay and Lesbian Family Service.* London: Institute of Family Therapy, 24–32 Stephenson Way, London NW1 2HX.

McGoldrick, M. (1982) 'Through the looking glass: Supervision of a trainee's "trigger" family.' In R. Whiffen and J. Byng-Hall (eds) *Family Therapy Supervision: Recent Developments in Practice.* London, Toronto and Sydney: Academic Press. New York and San Francisco: Grune and Stratton.

Parry, G. (1996) *NHS Psychotherapy Services in England: A Review of Strategic Policy.* NHS Executive. London: Department of Health.

Pegg, P. and Manocchio, A.J. (1982) 'In on the act.' In R. Whiffen and J. Byng-Hall (eds) *Family Therapy Supervision: Recent Developments in Practice.* London, Toronto and Sydney: Academic Press. New York and San Francisco: Grune and Stratton.

Rampage, C. (1994) 'Power, gender, and marital intimacy.' *Journal of Family Therapy 16*, 1, 139–143.

Reiss, D. (1989) 'The represented and practising family: Contrasting visions of family continuity.' In A. Samcroff and R. Emde (eds) *Relationship Disturbances.* New York: Basic Books.

Roth, A. and Fonagy, P. (1996) *What Works for Whom: A Critical Review of Psychotherapy Research.* New York: Guildford.

Selvini Palazzolli, M.S., Boscolo, L., Cecchin, G. and Prata, G. (1980) 'Hypothesising, circularity–neutrality: Three guidelines for the conductor of the session.' *Family Process 19*, 3–12.

Sluzki, C.E. (1978) 'Marital therapy from a systems theory perspective.' In T.J. Paolino and B.S. McCrady (eds) *Marriage and Marital Therapy: Psychoanalytic Behavioural and Systems Theory Perspectives.* New York: Brunner Mazel.

Thomas, L. (1995) 'Psychotherapy in the context of race and culture: An intercultural therapeutic approach.' In S. Fernando (ed) *Mental Health in a Multicultural Society.* London: Routledge.

Tomm, K. and Wright, L. (1982) 'Multilevel training and supervision in an outpatient service programme.' In R. Whiffen and J. Byng-Hall (eds) *Family Therapy Supervision: Recent Developments in Practice.* London, Toronto and Sydney: Academic Press. New York and San Francisco: Grune and Stratton.

Whiffen, R. (1982) 'The use of videotape in supervision.' In R. Whiffen and J. Byng-Hall (eds) *Family Therapy Supervision: Recent Developments in Practice.* London, Toronto and Sydney: Academic Press. New York and San Francisco: Grune and Stratton.

Whiffen, R. and Byng-Hall, J. (eds) (1982) *Family Therapy Supervision: Recent Developments in Practice.* London, Toronto and Sydney: Academic Press. New York and San Francisco: Grune and Stratton.

2

Agency-Based Family Therapy Training

An Account of the Experience of Setting Up and Running an Intermediate Level Family Training Clinic

Nuala Sheehan[1]

Live supervision of family therapy takes place in a variety of contexts, ranging from pairs to groups of colleagues providing peer consultation in a clinical setting, to the groups of advanced-level family therapy trainees working with a designated supervisor in a training institute. This chapter describes an agency-based family therapy training clinic which operated independently of any training establishment.[2] The training clinic aimed to provide intermediate-level clinical training to interdisciplinary groups of trainees working with professionals in training in district general hospitals with a designated supervisor over a period of one academic year. There is a growing need for this type of training opportunity as family therapy trainees are unlikely to accrue sufficient hours of supervised practice on accredited courses, as they are currently structured, to qualify for UKCP registration.[3] The shortfall could be made up by spending a year at post-qualifying advanced level in a similar, agency-based training clinic. Following the recent development in family therapy in Britain of the training of qualified family therapists as approved supervisors, increasing numbers of accredited supervisors will be available to run such training clinics. In addition to describing the expediencies and practicalities of setting up and running a training clinic, some contemporary theoretical and clinical issues concerning live supervision that emerge from the process of the evolution of the field of family therapy will be discussed.

---

1   Nuala Sheehan BA hons, APSW, Msc, MIFT is a UKCP registered family psychotherapist who is also a qualified psychiatric social worker. She provides an independent family psychotherapy service to primary care groups in Wiltshire and Somerset and works in private practice in Bath.

2   This has been the case from 1988, when the training clinic was set up, until 1995. In January 1995 the training clinic began taking trainees from the new intermediate level family therapy course at Bristol University which is largely practice based and which operates as a partnership between the University and the participating agencies.

3   Current AFT requirements at qualifying level as detailed in *The Blue Book* are 320 hours of supervised therapeutic practice to be completed in not less than two years and not more than five years.

Expedience and practicalities of setting up a training clinic

As family therapy is a relatively new therapeutic approach and a relatively new profession, there may be no precedent with a particular core profession or organisation for supporting and funding family therapy training, especially in areas where there are, as yet, no family therapy courses available.

This training clinic was based in a department of child and family psychiatry within a district general hospital, the Royal United Hospital in Bath. The former Bath District Health Authority was one of the first health authorities in the country to create family therapy posts. This occurred in 1987 when the former county of Avon Social Services Department deleted all of its psychiatric social work posts from departments of child and family psychiatry and child guidance clinics. In order to retain the services of two experienced social workers in the Bath hospital team, the health authority created family therapist posts. Both post holders subsequently undertook advanced family therapy training and became employees of the Bath Mental Health Care (NHS) Trust from its inception.

The issues of authority to run a training clinic and legitimisation of the work done by the team will vary from one context to another. There was an existing tradition of offering training in the multidisciplinary Bath team, which consisted of eight permanent professionals plus trainees in all disciplines. My links with the much larger adult psychiatric teams were maintained through academic meetings, where I had the opportunity to present systemic ideas in virgin territory, and through working with registrars in psychiatry who were on rotation. It became established practice that the registrar in our department would be a member of the family therapy training clinic, plus professional trainees from other disciplines. Knowledge of, and interest in, this training opportunity grew and spread to all disciplines within the hospital psychiatric services and to agencies outside the hospital, generating spontaneous applications for places in the clinic. In time, the process of advertising and recruitment became more formalised, selection criteria were raised and, in the new market economy, fees were charged to trainees from outside the Trust.

Any supervisor setting up a training clinic may well be, similarly, in a pioneering role, and would be wise to do some groundwork of networking and establishing credibility, both for the approach and for the project, with line managers from a variety of professions and agencies. The supervisor will also need to seek support for the project in her/his own agency and to ensure that the project is adequately equipped and resourced.[4] A fee for the training clinic will need to be decided, as well as starting and finishing dates. Publicity and application forms will need to be prepared several months in advance to allow time for recruitment and selection

---

4   Minimum requirements are: the guaranteed use of a suite of adequately sized rooms with a one-way screen; video equipment in good working order; a supply of videotapes; an earbug and/or a telephone link; an adequate supply of appropriate furniture for adults and children; and access to suitable toys and activities for children of all ages.

processes to be completed. Selection criteria will need to be established, depending on the level and mix of trainees required.[5]

My training clinic team met weekly for one session of three and a half hours, which allowed two families to be seen. The year was divided into three terms of 12 weeks each. I found the optimum number of trainees to be four; each trainee could expect to work with two or three families concurrently and this size of group allowed each trainee to accrue sufficient hours as therapist and observer. Suitable cases were selected from referrals to the team. I avoided cases where individual work was specifically requested or indicated as I do not think a team approach is suitable for individual work. I agree with Elsa Jones (Jones 1993) that it may feel overwhelming and intrusive to the individual client. However, it may be acceptable in cases where family or couple work develops into individual work and the client feels sufficiently engaged and comfortable with the team to continue to work with them. I also avoided cases where extensive liaison with other agencies or off-site work was likely, as these tend to be difficult to manage for trainees who are based elsewhere and are not available outside training clinic time. Of course, this aspect of the work cannot always be predicted, and it is important to discuss contingency arrangements with trainees as part of the contract of supervision. It is particularly important, I believe, that the supervisor avoids getting into direct contact with the client on behalf of the trainee wherever possible, as this is likely to be experienced by the trainee as undermining of her/his competence and her/his relationship with the client.

One way in which our practice evolved over time is that the training clinic came to write in advance to inform new clients of the set-up. Previously, clients had only learned about the team, the screen and video when they arrived for the first appointment. This shift was in line with the general shift in family therapy to a post-modern stance of becoming more open, more egalitarian and more collaborative in our relationships with clients (Anderson and Goolishian 1988; Hoffman 1993; White and Epston 1990). We invited clients to contact us in advance if they wished to discuss our way of working, so they had a genuine choice about whether or not to work with a team (see Appendix II). In practice, we found that very few families objected to our way of working and those who did could be offered an alternative within the agency. Another development was that we became more open about the fact that it was a training clinic and that, to some extent, the organisation of the clinic was for our benefit. Again, this has not had any deleterious consequences for the trainees' relationships with families, nor for families' willingness to attend. Families were invited to meet the team and to view the back-up room at the end of the first session.

5   I would recommend that trainees be expected to have at least completed an AFT-accredited introductory-level family therapy course, or to have had sufficient other training and experience to qualify for an intermediate-level course. Honorary contracts with the agency as well as individual and more detailed contracts of supervision between supervisor and trainee will need to be drawn up.

With the agreement of families, all sessions were videotaped, and trainees were required to review tapes between sessions and to take responsibility for planning the next session. Trainees were also required to write up each session to an agreed format and to take responsibility for letters and administration. The structure of the clinic allowed for pre-session discussion, within session interventions by earbug or telephone call-ins, time out discussion and a post-session debrief.

When clients did not attend, the time was used for video review and theoretical discussion. If necessary, time was booked for these activities occasionally instead of booking in a family. At the beginning of each year the group planned its own teaching programme and I circulated papers and books that we agreed to read. Specific topics were allocated to each trainee who was then responsible for a seminar presentation of the subject. A variety of teaching techniques were used, including role play.

Contemporary theoretical and clinical issues

A hallmark of the family therapy field is its self-reflective and evolving nature. The key papers on live supervision (e.g. Liddle and Schwartz 1983; Montalvo 1973; Schwartz, Liddle and Breunlin 1988) predate family therapy's contemporary post-modern or post-structuralist era, which challenges the idea that hidden structures exist within human groups (Hoffman 1993). As Lynn Hoffman states, 'the idea that systems and structures are merely convenient inventions casts doubt upon the entire systemic enterprise' (1993, p.104). The early papers on supervision advocate a stance of certainty and knowingness on the part of the supervisor. They use language such as 'the supervisor's demands' and 'a directive which must be followed' (Montalvo 1973), which, undoubtedly helpful in its time, is now discordant to the ears of family therapists who are struggling to abandon the expert position, to come from a position of not knowing and to be sensitive to the oppression which is embedded in language and practices we take for granted – what Foucault refers to as 'the micro-fascism of everyday life' (Rabinow 1984). Where does this leave the contemporary family therapy supervisor? If not paralysed into inactivity, how can we create a viable structure and a safe learning environment in harmony with these ideas so that our model of supervision is isomorphic with our model of therapy? To what extent can the endeavours of therapy and live supervision be genuinely co-constructed? As recently as 1992, Montalvo was quoted as saying that he believes responsible hierarchy is essential in therapy and in learning therapy (American Association for Marriage and Family Therapy 1992). Inevitably, there is a gap between therapy which can be 'pure' and practice which is multifaceted and 'adulterated'. It is my belief also that, if we are to avoid chaos and unproductive levels of anxiety for trainees, it is necessary to have some degree of planning, structure and benign leadership – these are the responsibility of the supervisor.

The supervisor is responsible for the quality of the clinical work, for meeting the learning needs of individual trainees and for the coherence of the training experience. I do not find it easy to define my model of therapy as I am aware of influences from a variety of models of therapy as disparate as psychodynamic therapy and structural family therapy. My preference is to draw on whatever style or technique seems to suit the situation. In line with Montalvo, I believe that the supervisor has a leadership role and that, when there is a conflict of interests between, say, the coherence of the team and the preferences of an individual trainee, the supervisor may be required to exercise authority. Wherever possible, I prefer to co-create solutions, to be open to learning from the trainees and to allow the team maximum scope to evolve its own practices and style.

Consider a situation where the trainee is Jack, a male, consultant psychiatrist, and the supervisor is Jill, a younger, female family therapist with a background in nursing. This scenario is not at all unusual, given that family therapy training in this country is currently only possible as a second professional training, that many trainees are well established in their core professions, and that advanced family therapy training, understandably, currently attracts more women from low status, female-dominated core professions than men from high status and more highly paid core professions. Whilst Jack has some basic training and experience of family therapy and has opted to undertake intermediate family therapy training in an agency-based training clinic set up by Jill, he has considerable anxiety about performing in the training clinic team. Jack expresses his anxiety in a reluctance to agree to the use of either the earbug or telephone call-ins. As Jill is an experienced supervisor, she has encountered such manifestations of anxiety in the past. She has learnt to identify and address these at the earliest possible stage by carefully negotiating a personal contract of supervision with each trainee individually. This provides an opportunity for Jack and Jill to be clear with each other about the nature of the supervisory relationship and the requirements of the trainee. When Jack's position emerges, he and Jill then have the opportunity to co-construct a solution to a potential problem. What they decide is that no interventions are to be made during the first session Jack has with a family, that they review the videotape of the session with the team and discuss interventions Jill might have made, that they practise using the earbug in a role play with the team and that Jack try using the earbug in his next session, with the expectation that he continue to use it. By being simultaneously respectful of Jack's position, willing to co-construct a solution and yet clear about a basic requirement of live supervision, Jill has taken charge and provided a structure within which it is possible for Jack to function and to develop.

As we move from 'power' to 'empowerment', from 'certainty' to 'curiosity' and from 'control' to 'collaboration' (Amundson, Stewart and Valentine 1993), it is important not to throw the baby out with the bath water and risk losing the rich source of perspectives and techniques that form the foundations of family therapy

(Hoffman 1981). However, equally important at this stage in our evolution as family therapists is our increasing openness to the integration of ideas from other disciplines and approaches, such as child development theories, cognitive-behavioural approaches, work with individuals and psycho-educational approaches (Sprenkle and Bischof 1994). In this climate of openness and collaboration, a multidisciplinary trainee group of individuals with a variety of personal and professional life experiences can be a valuable resource which can make a genuine multiple-voice contribution. The skill of the supervisor lies in the ability to both provide sufficient structure and planning to create a safe purposeful learning environment and simultaneously to adopt a stance of curiosity and not knowing which enables trainees to feel respected and free to contribute and to construct their own learning experience.

References

American Association for Marriage and Family Therapy (1992) *Supervision Bulletin.* Washington DC: AAMFT Publishing.

Amundson, J., Stewart, K. and Valentine, I. (1993) 'Temptations of power and certainty.' *Journal of Marital and Family Therapy 19,* 111–124.

Anderson, H. and Goolishian, H. (1988) 'Human systems as linguistic systems: Some preliminary and evolving ideas about the implications for clinical theory.' *Family Process 12,* 371–395.

Hoffman, L. (1981) *Foundations of Family Therapy.* New York: Basic Books.

Hoffman, L. (1993) *Exchanging Voices: A Collaborative Approach to Family Therapy.* London: Karnac Books.

Jones, E. (1993) *Family Systems Therapy: Developments in the Milan-Systemic Therapies.* Chichester: John Wiley and Sons.

Liddle, H.A. and Schwartz, R.C. (1983) 'Live supervision/consultation: Conceptual and pragmatic guidelines for family therapy training.' *Family Process 22,* 477–490.

Montalvo, B. (1973) 'Aspects of live supervision.' *Family Process 12,* 343–359.

Rabinow, P. (ed) (1984) *The Foucault Reader.* New York: Pantheon Press.

Schwartz, R.C., Liddle, H.A. and Breunlin, D.C. (1988) 'Muddles in live supervision.' In H.A. Liddle, D.C. Breunlin and R.C. Schwartz (eds) *Handbook of Family Therapy Training and Supervision 11.* New York: Guildford Press.

Sprenkle, D.H. and Bischof, G.P. (1994) 'Contemporary family therapy in the United States.' *Journal of Family Therapy 16,* 5–23.

White, M. and Epston, D. (1990) *Narrative Means to Therapeutic Ends.* New York and London: W.W. Norton and Company.

3

Supervisors, Therapists and Families: 'Fits' and Starts

Paul Blackburn[1]

This chapter is concerned with the interfaces between the supervisor, the therapist and the clinical family. It will consider some of the arguments for and against 'family of origin work' in family therapy training. In particular, it will focus on developmental/life-stage issues, for both the agency and the professional life of the workers involved, consideration of which is so important in understanding the effectiveness or ineffectiveness of working relationships in both clinical and professional contexts.

Dilemmas of 'fit': Agency considerations

Deciding to undertake an advanced training in clinical supervision may represent a significant point in the professional life of the would-be supervisor. The ease with which a context can be created in which to undertake this training may depend on the developmental stage of family therapy within the would-be supervisor's professional agency. If either party aims to achieve ownership of an 'advanced supervisor' status before the other is 'ready', difficulties (in an already difficult process) may become insurmountable.

My involvement with introductory- and intermediate-level family therapy training in my professional (NHS) agency over a number of years had a threefold significance. This training had engendered a certain family therapy 'culture and voice' which had been increasingly accepted by management. Second, this training had generated a significant reservoir of enthusiastic, if uncoordinated, intermediate-level trained staff. This staff group, involved in many areas of the

---

1   Paul H. Blackburn PhD is a family therapist in East Yorkshire. He is a member of the Institute of Family Therapy London and an honorary lecturer at the University of London.

Trust mental health services, sought supervision and guidance to improve and legitimise their practice. Finally, this training had created for me a certain professional profile within the agency which was, I suspect, significant in my negotiations with management to undertake an advanced training in clinical supervision. With demand and an educated management, my context was blessed with what, I would guess, were the necessary preconditions for this venture. One might say that the developmental stage of the agency was congruent with my professional development and there was a good enough 'fit' in this interface to maximise the chances of the endeavour.

As clinical supervisor of family therapy teams in both child and adult mental health, I was fortunate enough in having a number of more or less willing colleagues as fodder for my training. It should be emphasised, however, that these teams existed for the clinical services they provided and were not created for the purpose of this training. The training was seen as a way to enhance the quality of the clinical task.

Dilemmas of 'fit': The therapist's 'fit' with self and family of origin experience

The idea of 'fit' has traditionally been used in the family therapy world to describe how well a therapeutic 'reframe' or redefinition is likely to connect with the information from, and beliefs of, family members. The concept of 'fit' may also be used to describe the quality of the connection or interface between therapist and family. 'Fit' in this sense refers to: 'All those elements of personal style, wisdom, charisma and resourcefulness that give a psychologist the edge in introducing change to stuck systems' (Simon 1985, p.107).

Fit, then, Simon suggests, is clearly related to the process of joining (Minuchin 1974). Minuchin suggests that the process of joining is crucial in accessing a family's structure: 'The therapist's data and diagnoses are achieved experientially in the process of joining the family' (Minuchin 1974, p.89).

However, unlike joining, 'fit' involves no definable 'action'. Joining as a technique may be taught and learnt, whereas 'fit' (inevitably) happens.

The shift in thinking from a first-order perspective to a second-order position, which unites therapist and family as a therapeutic system, has introduced an important focus on the therapist/family interface. Considerations which will affect the quality of therapist/family fit are numerous, and may include culture (e.g. Falicov 1988; Schwartzman 1983); gender (e.g. Goldner 1985, 1987; Walters et al. 1988); life and family of origin experience (e.g. Bowen 1974; Byng-Hall 1985; Lieberman 1982); life cycle stage (e.g. Simon 1988); and even the therapist's sibling position (e.g. Toman 1976) in his/her family of origin.

It is self-evident to say that a therapist's family of origin experience (and all implied therein) will influence his/her style, personal repertoire and therefore, potentially, the 'fit' with a family. This experience will include how a therapist understands family structure, transgenerational influences and how rules and roles and so on evolve. The therapist's family of origin may be described both as a 'personal resource' (Lieberman 1980) aiding therapeutic skill or the cause of 'family of origin freeze' (McDaniel and Landau-Stanton 1991) which paralyses the therapist when he/she becomes overwhelmed by personal family issues triggered by particular clinical families.

However, the issues of whether and how to harness the influences inherent in a therapist's family of origin experience has divided professional opinion. A number of arguments have been offered to support the proposition that training family therapists should work on or with their families of origin. For example, McDaniel and Landau-Stanton (1991) suggests that family of origin work is a good way of teaching systemic thinking, enhances trainees' clinical competence and can be an 'insurance' against 'getting caught' with clinical families.

How one faces up to this 'responsibility' will, according to Lieberman (1982). vary according to one's theoretical position. The aims of family work from a Bowen position are: '1. To reverse emotional cutoffs. 2. To detriangle family members, 3. To increase differentiation of self. 4. To resist fusion' (Bowen 1987). Bowen suggests one should achieve these things in one's own family of origin if one is to be effective as a family therapist.

Lieberman's own 'transgenerational' position aims to: '1. Uncover secrets. 2. Cross generational boundaries. 3. Share unmourned losses. 4. Absorb and reconcile family culture differences' (see Lieberman 1980).

It may be argued that family of origin work would be important in identifying different relationships – 'scripts' and 'myths' (Byng-Hall 1985; Ferreira 1963; Stierlin 1973) – since even benign (i.e. non-problematic) family of origin patterns will impact on therapist/family fit. Byng-Hall conceptualised the script as a blueprint which organises family behaviours and interactions in particular contexts; it is like the script of a play which imbues the cast with a mental representation of all the relationships between the cast members. A therapist from a family with a maternal parenting script may 'fit' better or worse with a clinical family having a paternal parenting pattern according to how well or badly he/she is familiar with his/her parenting 'prejudice' (Cecchin 1992). Scripts can be described as 'replicative' or 'corrective'. For example, if a child's experience of being parented was good, he/she may be expected in adulthood to copy this model and to operate what Byng-Hall calls a replicative script. Conversely, if the experience was negative, he/she may attempt to correct the mistakes they perceived and exercise a corrective script. The application of replicative or (perhaps more significantly) corrective scripts in the therapist's own current family may need to be taken into account when assessing therapist family 'fit'.

However, including family of origin work in the training and/or supervision of family therapists raises a number of issues. McDaniel and Landau-Stanton (1991) suggest that as such work is likely to make trainees vulnerable to scrutiny by other trainees, an emphasis on the importance of group boundaries, confidentiality and safety is needed. Of equal interest is the question of how a distinction is maintained between family of origin 'work' and personal therapy. Where does one end and the other begin? McDaniel and Landau-Stanton (1991, p.464) list: '1. Shutting down and tightening up. 2. Rapid change in non-verbal behaviour. 3. Sudden subject change. 4. Pushing avoiding intensity inappropriately. 5. Forgetting out of sessions tasks.' These are the signals that personal issues are interfering with the functioning of the therapist and evidence that family of origin work is important for training therapists.

'Self-understanding' or skills development

Haley (1985, pp.173,179) takes the opposing view. He suggests: 'Training a student therapist can be conceived of as providing him with a rich philosophical life and helping him grow as an individual. Or can it be conceived of as teaching specific skills?' He concludes: 'The task is to teach therapy as a skill.' He goes as far as to say that a trainee should actively avoid institutions where the emphasis is placed on the personality and personal problems of the therapist rather than on skills to bring about change. Haley suggests that from his own experience the more personal therapy his trainees have had, the more difficult they become to teach. Furthermore, 'They become so preoccupied with themselves that clients have trouble getting their attention.' Haley is not suggesting that the therapist's family of origin experience will have no impact on his/her clinical competence or performance with certain families, but that the solution is for the therapist to develop better skills to work with the families which trigger personal issues. He gives, for example (1985), the case of a therapist who may have difficulty dealing with an authority figure such as a grandfather. Rather than encouraging the therapist to understand how he/she feels about authority figures and resolving it as personal problem, Haley suggests that the therapist should be trained in specific ways to deal with grandfathers, and to receive supervision on families containing authority figures. His contention is that family of origin work could seduce therapists into over-focusing on historical material rather than helping clients resolve their current dilemmas.

It would be interesting to speculate that Haley's therapist (above) may learn from clinical supervision how to deal with authority figures in his/her own family. If so, then in some way clinical supervision/skills training can facilitate a trainee's family of origin 'work' in much the same way as family of origin work aims to enhance clinical skills. There may be an isomorphism or circularity in these apparently dichotomous approaches which render partisan arguments for an exclusive approach less convincing.

In many instances the supervisor-in-training will have little or no remit to intrude upon or examine a supervisee's family of origin experience. Nevertheless, he/she may still maintain a focus on the 'fit' in terms of life cycle stage between the therapist and the clinical family. This focus provides three configurations, each with its own advantages and disadvantages, and each raising particular supervisory issues.

Dilemmas of 'fit': 'Configuring solutions'

1. 'The life cycle stages of family and therapist': The therapist has less life experience than key family members

First, take supervising the therapist/family system in which the therapist is not yet at the life cycle state of the family. In my experience, the therapist in this position often feels in a 'one-down' or less confident position. He/she may compensate by trying to sound too expert, or by joining inappropriately or with the wrong part of the family.

Similarly, the family may feel the therapist 'cannot know what it is like' and have less respect for, and confidence in, the therapist. An awareness of these pitfalls may be turned to advantage. For example, a great grandmother (Mrs S) was referred to a family therapy team with her problematic great grandson, who was resident with her. Problems deciding which team member should interview Mrs S were numerous. Two team members were (youngish) grandmothers themselves, and at first seemed logical choices for the therapist role. However, by instigating a pre-session discussion of these issues, it became apparent that the advantages inherent in their parenting experience risked generating a covert therapist/client competition as to who was the most competent mother. Consequently, the decision was made that the young unmarried and childless male team member should interview this great grandmother. This has the advantage of not only eliminating the risk of competition, but also providing a context for great respect, curiosity and positive connotation of past successes. Though the work was supervised 'live' by means of an earbug and one-way screen, it seemed to me that the most important part of the supervisory process in this case was in helping the therapist choose the appropriate stance in relation to the client. His position of curious deference provided a platform for helping this client generate her own solutions. Therapy was successfully completed, with the therapist thanking the client for helping him better understand families, the problems of parenting and of old age. The therapist's style was appropriate for this life cycle configuration. Clearly, being directive or more structural was less likely to be effective.

2. Dilemmas of 'fit': The therapist and key family members are in similar life cycle stages

When therapist and clinical family are at the same life cycle stage a useful 'fit' may be achieved more easily, since the family is more likely to feel the therapist can understand its problems, the therapist can empathise with family members and he/she is less likely to pathologise the family unnecessarily. A number of pitfalls remain, however. Supervision would be sensitive to the emotional triggers which may be present for the therapist or to the therapist becoming blinkered by his/her own (attempted) solutions to problems at the particular life stage. It may be that this is the life cycle configuration in which gender issues or inappropriate therapist/family member alliances are most likely to occur.

For example, a male therapist was recently observed to be unusually reluctant to 'hear' and discuss a mother's complaints and anxieties about her daughter's decision to 'take a year out' on an overseas voluntary service scheme. Indeed, the therapist felt my observations as supervisor to be misplaced until a video playback of the session improved his hindsight (!). Connecting the session with his and his wife's ambivalence and differences about their son having recently left home for university had the effect of liberating him to be more creative and to connect better with the family. In this particular life cycle configuration, supervision might focus on accepting multiplicity of possible solutions.

3. Dilemmas of 'fit': The therapist as 'senior expert' to key family members

When the therapist is beyond the life cycle stage of the clinical family the same array of pluses and pitfalls are present. Clearly, the therapist is less likely to be 'fazed' by any problem the family may display and family members are more likely to feel understood. The therapist is likely to have his/her own problem-solving experience and a 'fund of personal anecdotes' (Simon 1985). He/she is harder to disqualify and may generate more confidence than in other configurations. There is, however, a danger that the family feels undermined by a 'too expert' therapist, who risks becoming less curious or distant and patronising. He/she may tend to 'lecture' and generate dependency. The clinical family may awaken 'ancient ghosts and curses' (Simon 1985) in the therapist. This is the life cycle configuration in which being directive or structural is most likely to be effective.

Finding a 'fit': General observations

Simon (1988) offers a number of considerations aimed at helping therapists find a 'fit' with families:

1. Choosing a stance (one up/one down).

2. Choosing a model (Milan, Structural, etc.), both according to the ages of the therapist and family.

3. Choosing a supervisor, not on the basis of clinical experience, but with the intention of complementing the life experience of the therapist.

4. Networking, which may be seen as an alternative form of supervision, since it allows therapists to interact with other professionals of varying ages, gender, ethnicity, etc., who see the world through different lenses.

Like Lieberman and McGoldrick, Simon emphasises the importance of the rigorous study of one's family of origin.

This is a brief and incomplete review of some of the arguments which have evolved from the consideration of the impact of a therapist's own family, and the supervision issues inherent in its interface with clinical families. It may be incomplete for many reasons, but not least for the fact that the inclusion of a supervisor in the therapeutic system adds a whole new layer of 'fit' and increases possible life cycle configurations (supervisor–therapist–family) manyfold.

Many (if not all) of the above issues apply equally well to the supervisor/ supervisee 'fit' as they do to the therapist/clinical family interface. 'Stuckness' in therapy may, therefore, reflect a bad 'fit' in either (or both) relationship(s). In this, the supervisor has a responsibility to explode the myth that he/she has 20:20 therapeutic vision.

References

Bowen, M. (1974) 'Towards the differentiation of self in one's own family of origin.' In F. Andrews and P. Loris (eds) *Georgetown Symposia Papers*. Washington DC: Georgetown University Press.

Bowen, M. (1987) *Family Therapy in Clinical Practice*. Norsvale, New Jersey: Jason Aronssen.

Byng-Hall, J. (1985) 'The family script: A useful bridge between theory and practice.' *Journal of Family Therapy 7*, 301–305.

Cecchin, G. (1992) Unpublished address to a psychology conference, York University.

Falicov, C.J. (1995) 'Training to think culturally: A multidimensional comparative framework'. *Family Process 34*, 4, 373–389.

Ferreira, A.J. (1963) 'Family myths: The covert rules of the relationship.' *Archives of General Psychiatry 9*, 457–463.

Goldner, V. (1985) 'Feminism and family therapy.' *Family Process 24*, 31–47.

Goldner, V. (1987) 'Instrumentalism, feminism and the limits of family therapy.' *Journal of Family Psychology 1*.

Haley, J. (1985) *Problem Solving Therapy*. New York: Harper and Row.

Lieberman, S. (1980) *Transgenerational Family Therapy*. London: Croom Helm.

Lieberman, S. (1982) 'Going back to your own family.' In R. Whiffen and J. Byng-Hall (eds) *Family Therapy Supervision: Recent Developments in Practice*. London: Academic Press.

McDaniel, S.H. and Landau-Stanton, J. (1991) 'Family-of-origin work and family therapy skills training.' *Both-And Family Process 30*, 459–470.

Minuchin, S. (1974) *Families and Family Therapy*. Cambridge, Mass: Harvard University Press.

Minuchin, S., Rosman, B. and Baker, L. (1978) *Psychosomatic Families*. Cambridge, Mass: Harvard University Press.

Schwartzman, J. (1983) 'Family ethnography: A tool for clinicians.' In C.J. Falicov (ed) *Cultural Perspectives in Family Therapy*. Rockville: MD Aspen.

Simon, R.M. (1988) 'Families life cycle issues in the therapy system.' In E. Carter and M. McGoldrick (eds) *The Changing Family Life Cycle: A Framework for Family Therapy*, 2nd Edition. New York: Gardner Press.

Stierlin, H. (1973) 'Group fantasises and family myths: Some theoretical and practical aspects.' *Family Process 12*, 111–125.

Toman, W. (1976) *Family Constellation*. New York: Springer.

Walters, M., Carter, B., Papp, P. and Silverstein, O. (1988) *The Invisible Web: Gender Patterns in Family Relationships*. New York and London: Guildford.

4

From Here to Eternity and Back Again
Developing a Supervisory Relationship with Training Family Therapists

Damian McCann

Introduction

Family therapy as an area of study and practice within the UK has, over the past twenty years, developed into a recognised profession with qualified practitioners occupying specific family therapy posts within the public, private and voluntary sectors. The formalisation of training of family therapists has correctly resulted in a new focus on the training of the trainers, and hence the emergence of postgraduate courses leading to the accreditation of supervisors. This developmental shift within the profession adds a further layer of formalisation and supposed expertise, which is likely to influence the future shape and direction of family therapy in this country.

In this chapter, the nature of the supervisory relationship within a training context will be explored. Tensions inherent in supervising trainees at different stages of development will be addressed. As discussed in Chapters 1 and 2, recent developments within systemic practice, particularly those associated with a postmodern position, are challenging more traditional models of supervision. It is argued, however, that in the early stages of training, it may be more helpful to draw on established approaches that provide greater structure and direction, rather than relying on those that value uncertainty and multiple perspectives.

The nature of the supervisory relationship

In undertaking the task of supervision, it seems imperative that aspiring supervisors have in their minds some idea of what it means to be a supervisor and, more importantly, the particular ingredients that distinguish supervisors from qualified practitioners. Do supervisors adorn a new set of clothes, or is it merely the case that practitioners grow into their existing clothes enough to feel that they have some learning to impart?

In attempting to answer this question, Jones (1995) makes the point that there is a general agreement among all schools of family therapy that training and therapy are similar in structure, or isomorphic, and that similar theoretical considerations apply to each. She goes on to suggest that 'ideas about how people change, and the trainer's style of functioning with trainees will give information about how she works with clients and vice versa' (p.187). Attention is therefore drawn to the importance and coherence of the trainer's model of therapy and functioning within the supervisory relationship. This would seem to imply, therefore, that practitioners do indeed need to grow into their existing clothes as part of the journey to become a supervisor.

Other practitioners, such as Heath (1982) or Schwartz, Liddle and Breunlin (1988), have highlighted additional components and, in particular, the requirement on supervisors that they occupy a clear hierarchical position as expert teacher and trainer. Each of these authors hold the supervisor responsible, not only for the teaching of specific skills, but also that this must be done in ways that ultimately foster trainee competence and independence. Schwartz, Liddle and Breunlin (1988), for example, likened the supervisory relationship to the master/ apprentice model of learning, and Gershenson and Cohen (1978) visualised the hierarchies of the supervisory relationship in terms of the trainee's development. This would seem to be implying something more than clinical experience on the part of the supervisors; but the extent to which supervisors occupy and foster such a hierarchical position may have more to do with the supervisor's model of therapy and theoretical orientation than any preordained requirement on the part of supervisors to be 'the expert' in relation to trainees. To really understand this point, however, it is necessary to contextualise the ideas within an evolving field. For instance, those who were influencing thinking and practice in the 1970s and early 1980s, whether they were practising within the structural, strategic or Milan schools of therapy, were all operating within a first-order cybernetic frame. Such a frame emphasises the expertise of the therapist who, it is assumed, is able to stand outside the family system, locate the dysfunction and apply interventions that will effect major transformation, referred to as second-order change (Watzlawick, Beavers and Jackson 1967). The confidence and certainty with which practitioners operated in the 1970s, and the skills they used to execute therapy, impacted systemically on the training of family therapists, and is also evidenced in the writings of those around this period, especially those advocating strict hierarchical positions in which one generation hands on their wisdom to the next. However, holding onto the belief that supervisors require something more than clinical experience and are not simply clones of those who trained them, it should be possible, returning to the clothes analogy, to choose one's additional garments from a range of options rather than sticking to a uniform, for a uniform, although identifiable, may be quite restrictive in terms of creativity and initiative.

First-order training and post-modernist approaches

Jones (1995) suggests that a first-order trainer operating from a model consistent with a first-order approach may intervene frequently and directly in a trainee's work, the assumption being that this is a useful way of teaching trainees therapy. The thinking behind this action is that the trainee must be taught the necessary skills and techniques to undertake ethically appropriate and effective therapy. It is therefore the job of the supervisor to impart this knowledge and expertise to the training therapist. Haley (1996) likens this process to learning how to drive a car. He reminds us that there are consequences if one does it badly, and argues that it is best 'to have an experienced driver sit with the beginner for driving practice, ready to take over if there is difficulty on the street' (p.vii). He goes on to say that 'beginners are taught the rules of the road as well as the skills involved in driving the vehicle' (p.vii). The emphasis within a first-order framework, therefore, is that of teaching trainees the art and skill of practice.

By contrast, instructive interaction for post-modernists 'cuts little ice'. Here the focus is on the discussion outside the main body of the session with the aim of inviting the trainee to consider alternative hypotheses and styles of interaction. Jones (1995) believes that this reflects the viewpoint put forward by Cecchin and Fruggeri (1986), that there can be a significant difference between teaching techniques as opposed to teaching a way of thinking. Adopting a more reflexive position, such as that outlined by Andersen (1987), in which the supervisor, singly or in the presence of the team behind the screen, offers reflections in front of the therapist and family, questions further the centrality of the supervisor's position. Here the reflections, which are speculative in nature, are designed to perturb the therapeutic system by creating new ideas, which may or may not be taken up by the family and interviewer.

Shifting further from the position of supervisor as expert to one that is more consistent with a post-modern position (in which knowledge is socially con-structed and where there is an enduring reflectivity, the authenticity of multiple voices, and uncertainty) has enormous implications for the supervisory relation-ship. To begin with, since there is no objective reality or truth, the supervisor is seen only as an expert in an exploratory conversational process with the supervisee, in the shaping of the supervisee's narrative. In other words, it is a generative conversation, in which the supervisee is, according to Anderson and Swim (1995), 'the expert in his or her own life, narratives, and experiences' (p.2). The supervisee is also regarded as 'an active architect of personal learning goals (p.2), trusted in his or her capacity for self-solution, agency, and learning' (p.3). In addition, the shared inquiry within this post-modern framework is regarded as the critical interaction where, as Anderson and Swim put it, 'the familiar, i.e. the problem as defined by the supervisee, is co-explored and where learning evolves from a co-exploration of the new' (p.1). Such a stance, however, requires a degree of uncertainty, which most supervisors may experience as deeply uncomfortable and which embodies particular dilemmas when evaluation and clinical accountability are incorporated back into the supervisory task.

Establishing the training clinic

1. Membership of the training team

The training clinic was set up within the Department of Child and Adolescent Psychiatry in Middlesex where I am employed as Principal Family Therapist. It was a requirement of the course I was undertaking to establish such a clinic, as this provided my own training base as well as a training setting for family therapists. At the time of writing, there were three trainees, two of whom were students outside of the department. They had completed an intermediate training in family therapy and needed to gain the relevant clinical hours in preparation for the final stages of their training in family therapy.

The third, a senior registrar in child psychiatry, was seeking a more formalised systemic experience in working with families. I should perhaps mention at this juncture that all three trainees were white females being supervised by a white male in a context in which there was a strong adherence to hierarchical relationships and structures, since all these factors were impacting on the task in hand.

2. Ingredients of a comprehensive training programme

A comprehensive training programme, according to Hodas (1985), frequently utilises both live and videotape supervision as a means of maximising therapeutic learning. Whilst running the training clinic, I had use of video recording facilities, a one-way screen and earbug. Hodas also points out that these forms of supervision tend to be mutually reinforcing, since what is learned during live supervision, i.e. where the supervisor is positioned behind the one-way screen and has access to the trainee therapist working with the family by means of telephone contact or earbug, not only influences subsequent performance during the next session, but also increases the therapist's application of him/herself as an agent of change. This is also a major focus of videotape supervision, which provides an opportunity for considering alternatives for change without the pressures of the therapeutic moment. Essentially, the videotape supervision offers both trainee and supervisor the opportunity of tracking each other's thinking in relation to the therapeutic session as it unfolds. The reflection offered by videotape supervision also, according to Hodas, increases the therapeutic leverage at the same time as improving conceptual clarity. In addition, both trainee and supervisor can use the videotape supervision to clarify plans for the next session.

A further component of a comprehensive training programme is the shift away from working with individual trainees to working with small groups of trainees. Hodas believes that group context for training maximises learning potential, since the training therapists can learn, both by doing and watching others. Heath (1982) suggests that trainees benefit from the group context by finding reassurance in the difficulties other members have in working with families. In spite of these obvious advantages, difficulties do arise, and tensions exist within the training context which are well documented in the literature.

3. The structure of the therapy session

As has been mentioned earlier, one of the main aims of supervision is to help the training family therapist maximise his/her skills, which also implies a clear grasp of theory underpinning such practices. The extent to which supervisors structure the training context, and the extent to which they work with trainees with a more reflexive space, will influence greatly the training and therapeutic work undertaken within the training context. For example, as a family therapist working with post-modern ideas where, curiosity, reflexivity and second-order cybernetics (i.e. the therapist as part of the system), are much in evidence, I naturally approached the task of supervision with a high degree of collaboration and openness. In practice, this meant that I encouraged the group, myself included, to generate pre-session ideas prior to the therapist meeting the family. The trainee would then be asked to consider which of the ideas was felt to be most helpful to his/her thinking and how he/she might begin the session. My role, in collaboration with the other voices behind the one-way screen, was to offer thoughts and suggestions directly to the trainee though the earpiece. The interventions would, consistent with a post-modern framework, be offered in such a way as to allow the trainee therapist the opportunity of taking these ideas up if they fitted with his/her thinking, or to ignore them if they did not. At the very least they connected the trainee, therapist and team behind the screen and offered a possible perturbation to the trainee's work with the family.

Consistent with the original Milan team's development of systemic thinking and practice, the session is classically divided into five sections: pre-session (as mentioned earlier), for discussion of referral information or a summary of the previous session, and for the elaboration of hypotheses; the bulk of the interview between therapist and clients; the inter-session consultation, where therapist and team share and elaborate ideas; the final part of the session, where the therapist returns to the family in order to explore these ideas further, or give them a task or ritual to perform between sessions; and the post-session discussion between therapist and team (Jones 1995, p.12). Structuring the session in this way offers all concerned, including the family, access to thinking as the therapy progresses. It should by definition, also, offer some built-in protection against a trainee veering too far off the track.

4. Clinical dilemmas in supervising trainees from the training clinic

In spite of the safeguards listed above, problems were encountered by the author in supervising a student who, having had some recent teaching on the narrative approach, ventured into new and unexpected territory. During the interview, she began to talk with an enuretic child and his family about 'Mr Accident' catching him out. As the training supervisor watching this interview, I was faced with a number of dilemmas. Should I call the trainee out and clarify the goals? Should I let her continue, given that the enuretic child seemed to be engaging with the approach and she seemed to know what she was doing? In the event, I sat watching, but the approach was difficult to sustain given that a clear marital issue was beginning to emerge in the work with this family. At this point, I discussed with the trainee more familiar ways in which she might help the couple begin to tackle this issue. For instance, we offered the couple the opportunity of being seen together as parents to think about useful strategies for tackling their son's difficulty. Dealing with this shift in thinking could have been more difficult had the trainee not been so willing to abandon the narrative approach. In that event, the trainee and I would have had to clarify the future goals of therapy and carefully plot the stages and development of the narrative through subsequent sessions.

Tensions also emerged in other work, where I felt that the trainee was not 'properly engaging' with a mother who was struggling to control her children and who was feeling exposed and persecuted by the very sessions that were designed to help her. Although I knew exactly what I would have done as a therapist, occupying a different position, i.e. that of trainee supervisor, left me as helpless as the trainee in the face of this challenging piece of work. Attempts to impart my thinking seemed only to confuse and paralyse still further the trainee in her work with the family. However, following a routine observation by the course consultant where she saw first hand my supervision of the trainee struggling with the family, we were able to review my role as supervisor within this process. Through this consultation it became apparent that I had failed to structure the training clinic sufficiently to establish a clear role for myself as supervisor and to provide enough direct guidance for the trainees in their work with families. By providing a clearer structure, the trainee was in a better position to assist the mother in developing more appropriate boundaries for her children.

The impact of the trainee's stage of development on the supervisory process

Schwartz, Liddle and Breunlin (1988) suggest that trainees at different levels of skills development need to be treated differently. Gershenson and Cohen (1978) propose a three-stage model of development for trainees that links closely with that proposed by Berger and Dammann (1982):

Stage 1

Here the trainee exhibits anxiety in meeting with families and performing well in front of his/her supervisor and the other members of the training team. Often trainees at this stage of development report not being able to fully understand how interventions are constructed and, as a result, may appear reticent about implementing suggestions and interventions offered by the supervisor. Although this changes over time, usually in response to the trainee feeling attached to what John Byng-Hall (1995) refers to as a 'secure base' where risks can be taken, the shift is only partial.

Stage 2

At this stage, the trainee understands the construction and logic of interventions, but struggles to carry them out within the session. Trainees at this stage may also be exhibiting what Schwartz refers to as 'robotisation'. This is the process whereby trainees mechanically carry out the supervisor's every command with little initiative or creativity. In spite of this, supervisors and trainees at this stage of development may notice a reduced verticality in their relationship as they shift towards working more as a team.

Stage 3

This represents the highest level of development, and at this stage the trainee thinks systemically and uses that thinking in their work with families. They will, for instance, show an ability to design and implement systemic interventions themselves rather than relying on the supervisor to do this for them.

I would argue that the same developmental processes apply equally to the training supervisor, who, in the early stages of the transition from experienced therapist to supervisor, exhibits the same tentative, insecure and anxious responses as the beginning family therapist. However, whereas the training family therapist tends to 'dry up' in family meetings, the practising supervisor, by contrast, has a propensity to intervene more and make many detailed suggestions over the phone or earbug to the trainee, or even enter the room and take over the session.

Although this may be welcomed by the struggling trainee, it constitutes first-order change and, if left unattended, has the potential for blocking further development in the supervisory relationship. The training supervisor is essentially faced with the challenge of creating a space for trainees to learn new skills in working with families, and of doing so in a way that does not underestimate, or unduly protect the trainee from the stress of struggling beyond, their developmental threshold to new levels of competence. At the same time, the training supervisor must assume responsibility for developing immediate goals and priorities for interventions as the session unfolds. Hodas (1985) suggests that the supervisor will be trying to ensure a successful outcome to the session, so that if a therapist is doing well, the supervisor will not intervene, or will only do so to suggest a refinement of technique. If, on the other hand, the trainee therapist is faltering, the supervisor is activated and may call in on a number of occasions, invite the therapist out or join the therapist in the room to regain control of the session.

Inherent in this discussion is a clear responsibility on the part of the supervisor to protect the family from the inadequacies of the beginning therapist. Montalvo (1973) suggests that live supervision has the advantage of ensuring that one does not have to wait until the damage has been done before attempting to repair events. By having a more experienced person observing and orienting the process while it is happening, major pitfalls can be avoided, and those that cannot be avoided can be more easily corrected. The extent to which trainees and families are exposed to 'damage' of any description is, I feel, one of the major tensions inherent in the supervisory relationship, particularly in live work with families.

Discarding most of these concerns, a number of authors, such as Anderson and Swim (1995), Turner and Fine (1995) and Stewart and Amundson (1995), offer convincing arguments for working with trainees within a post-modern framework.

The contribution of post-modern approaches

Supervision viewed as a 'collaborative conversation that is generative and relational, through which supervisees create their own answers, and in doing so experience freedom and self-confidence' (Anderson and Swim 1995, p. 1), offers a useful counterpoint to the more traditional narratives outlined above. Consistent with the notion that there is no absolute truth, supervisors within this model are viewed more as 'mentors' than as 'experts'. Uncertainty and unpredictability, the two vital ingredients that bring this model to life, leave ample space for exploration and the potential for developing shared meanings. However, a distinction needs to be drawn between an active position of uncertainty, as a means for opening a collaborative conversation, and simple empty-headedness that, after all, could be deeply unsettling to a trainee therapist and the supervisory relationship in general. In essence, the conversation taking place between the supervisor and the supervisee is part of an open and ongoing exploration of new meanings and understandings, and to some extent mirrors the therapeutic conversation taking place between the trainee and the family. Within this approach, there is an expectation that the supervisor will abandon efforts to teach or instruct the trainee and instead will attempt to perturb the trainee's development by offering knowledge, observations and suggestions. The supervisor, being part of the system, will also be affected and altered by the feedback from the trainee and will as such be open to new learning within the supervisory endeavour.

The struggle to incorporate these ideas into practice and the dilemmas inherent in doing so should not be underestimated. For instance, lately, I have been wondering if my own reflections, consistent in style with Andersen's 'reflecting team dialogue', outlined earlier in this chapter, are actually a covert attempt by me to control the session, since these reflections have come at times when I have been most concerned with the direction of the session. Also, the act of entering the room and sharing these ideas, however tentative they may be, could be construed by the training therapist and the family as a subtle undermining of the therapist's authority in relation to working with the family. The power inherent in my gender, race and position as supervisor also complicates further the relationship between the therapist and the family and should not be ignored in the supervisory intervention.

Although Anderson and Swim acknowledge the difficulty in operationalising this approach (schooled as we are in the need for clear and certain thinking), they nevertheless offer very little guidance, other than to encourage supervisors and therapists to share continually their work with each other. Their belief is that a shared exploration of the new is sufficient in itself to bring about change and development. However, issues of safe and unsafe practice remain largely unaddressed, and it remains to be seen whether it is possible to unite the seemingly incompatible stances of authority and collaboration within the supervisory role.

Developing this argument further, Turner and Fine (1995) attempt to address the thorny issue of evaluation within a post-modern framework. 'Whether in the therapy room or in the supervision session, we encourage those who have previously had less authority to speak and we value the diversity their voices provide' (p.57). Traditionally, evaluation in the family therapy field has inferred the modernist notion that the supervisor/evaluator can and will measure what the therapist knows as though learning can be quantified and measured objectively. Turner and Fine's solution to this dilemma from a post-modern perspective, where anyone who participates has some possibility of influencing the outcome, is to openly acknowledge the power and control supervisors have in the evaluative position accorded by registering bodies. The authors believe that such transparency leads to increased challenges from therapists about the judgements made by supervisors, which in turn expands the evaluation dialogue and allows for new perspectives to emerge. In addition, they suggest a similar opening up of the final reports on trainees by the inclusion of multiple voices, including that of the trainee. Although this offers some comfort to those wishing to develop a more collaborative relationship between supervisors and therapists, it does not, however, address the central dilemmas facing every supervisor – namely, that of deciding whether to pass, fail or defer trainees. This is all the more important given that training institutions are under pressure to demonstrate that trainees have met the strict criteria laid down for successful completion of the training.

For me, the central issue is one of developing collaborative relationships that do not blunt the cutting edge of therapy or indeed provide safe hiding places for unsafe practitioners. Stewart and Amundson (1995) argue that the processes of supervision themselves participate in the definition of family therapy as a profession, and as such should be conducted within a framework of ethics that defines who we are and how we should be. Their strategy in working with trainees is to present them with a number of ethical dilemmas and not attempt to apply some fixed solution to the problem. The same must also apply to supervisors, especially when they are faced with trainees who are failing. In other words, if the supervisor is working within a post-modern frame, is it his/her ethical duty to fail the student or is it necessary to keep the dialogue open? Until the dominant discourse of training, implying some notion of success or failure, shifts, we as supervisors, whatever our frame of reference, must not shirk our responsibility of ensuring some agreed standard of practice for ourselves, our trainees and, most of all, for the families with whom we work.

Conclusion

This chapter has considered two quite distinct approaches relating to the supervision of trainee family therapists. Supervisor A, for instance, holds with the belief that supervision is concerned with teaching skills and imparting knowledge in a clear and authoritative manner. The task of the supervisor in this process is to teach trainees the necessary skills and techniques to undertake ethically appropriate and effective therapy. Supervisor B, on the other hand, is more concerned with developing a collaborative conversation in which reflections offered before, during and after the therapy session facilitate change and development. Less emphasis is placed on structure and more on co-constructing new meanings through dialogue. The more open the dialogue, the greater the potential for change. The extent to which it is possible, however, to combine these two seemingly incompatible approaches remains open to debate. In the meantime, it is suggested that trainees in the very early stages of training experience difficulty making use of generative and collaborative conversations as a basis for practice, and therefore benefit more from a pragmatic approach in which there is a high degree of structure and supervisory input. A tight corset may be preferable to the emperor's new clothes, but trainees in the later stages of development will need more space and encouragement to experience and find their own unique style and approach, and to that end therapy conducted within a post-modern framework may have much to offer. At the centre of this debate is of course the families with whom we work. They, after all, provide the fertile ground on which trainees and supervisors develop a dynamic practice relationship. No doubt, the positioning and coordinating of these key players will continue to exercise the field for some considerable time to come.

References

Andersen, T. (1987) 'The reflecting team: Dialogue and meta-dialogue in clinical work.' *Family Process 24*, 4, 415–428.

Anderson, H. and Swim, S. (1995) 'Supervision as collaborative conversation: Connecting the voices of supervisor and supervisee.' *Journal of Systemic Therapies 14*, 2, Summer 1995.

Berger, M. and Dammann, C. (1982) 'Live supervision as context, treatment, and training.' *Family Process 21*, 337–344.

Byng-Hall, J. (1995) *Rewriting Family Scripts: Improvisation and Systems Change.* New York: The Guildford Press.

Cecchin, G. and Fruggeri, L. (1986) 'Consultation with mental health systems in Italy.' In L. Wynne, C. Lyman, S. McDaniel, H. Swan, G. Weber and T. Timothy (eds) *Systems Consultation: A New Perspective for Family Therapy.* New York: The Guildford Press.

Gershenson, J. and Cohen, M. (1978) 'Through the looking glass: The experience of two family therapy trainees with live supervision.' *Family Process 17*, 225–230.

Haley, J. (1976) 'Problems of training family therapists.' In J. Haley (ed) *Problem Solving Therapy.* Jossey Bass.

Haley, J. (1996) *Learning and Teaching Therapy.* Guildford.

Heath, A. (1982) 'Team family therapy training: Conceptual and pragmatic considerations.' *Family Process 1982*.

Hodas, G. (1985) 'A systems perspective on family therapy supervision.' In Grune and Stratton (1985) *Adjunctive Techniques in Family Therapy.*

Jones, E. (1995) 'Family systems therapy.' In *The Milan Systemic Therapies.* Wiley.

Montalvo, B. (1973) 'Aspects of live supervision.' *Family Process 12*.

Schwartz, R., Liddle, H. and Breunlin, D. (1988) 'Muddles in live supervision.' In H. Liddle, *et al. Handbook of Family Therapy Training and Supervision.* New York: Guildford Press.

Stewart, K. and Amundson, J. (1995) 'The ethical post-modernist: Or not everything is relative all at once.' *Journal of Systemic Therapies 14*, 2, Summer 1995.

Turner, J. and Fine, M. (1995) 'Post-modern evaluation in family therapy supervision.' *Journal of Systemic Therapies 14*, 2, Summer, 57–69.

Watzlawick, P., Beavers, J.H. and Jackson, D. (1967) *Pragmatics of Human Communication: A Study of Interactional Patterns, Pathologies, and Paradoxes.* New York: W.W. Norton.

5

The Trainee Perspective

Damian McCann and Gwynneth Down

Introduction

This book would not be complete without incorporating the perspectives and voices of the trainees involved. This has been achieved through two separate but related interviews, in which a trainee of Down was interviewed by McCann and one of McCann's trainees was similarly interviewed by Down. These were one-off interviews, lasting approximately one hour, and were conducted retrospectively after the trainees had completed their training. They were designed to highlight strengths and possible pitfalls of trainee family therapists working as part of trainee supervisory teams with two supervisors who were themselves in training.

In this chapter, trainees' views on their supervised clinical training are explored. Issues discussed include the settings, working out responsibilities for learning, contracts within the training setting, addressing issues of power and difference, and the experiences of working in the training teams under different methods of supervision.

The setting

Both trainees were part of a training family therapy workshop in two separate departments of child and adolescent psychiatry. **A** was already employed as a social worker within the department and was undertaking further training in family therapy. **B**, on the other hand, was in private practice as a counsellor and hypnotherapist and had sought the placement to underpin her training in family therapy. **A** is a black British woman and **B** is a white UK-born woman.

Both supervisors were employed as family therapists in their respective settings and were, as discussed in the previous chapters, in training to become approved supervisors of family therapists. For Down, the family therapy workshop fitted well with the general ethos of the child psychiatry department in which she worked, itself being part of a London teaching hospital, whereas for McCann, the training clinic was only approved by the lead consultant as part of his training to become a qualified supervisor. This may have played a part in the overall feeling of independence and autonomy which occupied both supervisors in their respective settings. McCann's trainee, for example, commented that there were times during her placement when particular pressures within the service resulted in the team leader (a consultant child psychiatrist) questioning whether she could justify McCann's time as a trainer rather than as a therapist. This was particularly so once McCann had completed his supervisory training, and in turn raises questions concerning the extent to which trainees should be cushioned or exposed to pressures internal to the setting in which the placement is conducted. This also touches on a fundamental issue concerning the degree of responsibility – both clinical and professional – that the supervisor assumes within the setting and the extent to which she/he may be accountable to other professionals; for example, the consultant child psychiatrist/team leader.

Both supervisors operated an open training group, meaning that students came and went during the life of the group. This had important implications for group cohesion and coherence, and was particularly pertinent for those trainees who stayed in the group for several years. **A**, for example, joined Down's family therapy workshop in 1994. At that stage, there were two trainees, although this increased to four in 1995. **B**, on the other hand, was the only trainee when she joined McCann's workshop, and over the next three years had to cope with a variety of trainees coming and going. The particular issues relating to group dynamics will be discussed in more detail as the chapter unfolds.

Aims and objectives

The family therapy workshops in both clinics were established to meet the following aims and objectives:

- to offer a specific training in systemic thinking and practice
- to provide opportunities for developing skills under direct supervision from qualified family therapists (it is likely in the future that practitioners offering this service must also possess an appropriate supervisory qualification)
- to extend thinking and practice generally through group discussions, the use of genograms, videotape supervision and a consideration of issues arising during the course of training linked to theoretical papers.

The contract

It is generally recognised that contracts are a fundamental prerequisite for any trainee undertaking a placement in a therapeutic setting (Carroll 1996; Feltham and Dryden 1994). As with contracts of employment, placement contracts also provide a framework and structure for practice. (For a more detailed consideration of the factors involved in establishing trainee placements for family therapists – some of which have relevance to the drafting of contracts – the reader is referred to Appendix IV.)

Two points of general interest emerged in regard to the contract for training that both supervisors established with their respective students. First, **B** was issued with an honorary contract of employment, whereas **A**, by virtue of her permanent employment within the department, did not require such a contract. Of importance is the need to separate contracts of employment from placement or training contracts, since they are of a different order and are usually designed for a quite different purpose.

Second, although Down established a contract outlining the learning object-ives with **A**, this was perceived, at least by **A**, as Down's responsibility. In other words, Down was seen as the one in charge of the placement and was held responsible for reviewing and keeping track of what happened during the life of the workshop. Although indeed this may be appropriate, it does raise questions concerning the position of the trainee with regard to collaboration and involving him/herself in establishing learning objectives and being actively involved in reviewing the placement.

Addressing issues of power and difference

The essential difference between the two placements was that of establishing ground rules at the beginning of training as a basis for proactively tackling issues of power and difference, and addressing these as and when they emerged through the clinical work. In many respects these can be viewed as opposite ends of a continuum, but it is likely that Down's stance in initiating ground rules for the group helped to establish a clearer, and to some extent safer, framework for thinking and practice. Included in this discussion were rules relating to confident-iality, respecting different points of view and giving permission to challenge oppressive and discriminatory practice. In addition, the group, on a number of occasions, discussed a variety of papers relevant to gender, power, race and ethnicity.

Although none of these issues were ignored or avoided in McCann's super-vision group, the discussions were primarily related to specific families and the issues they brought into the work, rather than to the therapist/supervisor system. Given the composition of the group, which at one stage, in addition to **B**, included a trainee counselling psychologist and two trainees in child psychiatry, **B** subsequently felt that it might have been helpful to address the relative power positions within the group as dynamics relating to a perceived hierarchy began to emerge. At issue is the ways in which this could have been raised in the group.

It is worth noting that sexuality was not formally discussed in either training group. **A** recalled a discussion about gay and lesbian relationships linked to a paper on domestic violence, but agreed that the group had not really opened a fuller discussion on the impact of sexuality on the work.

Ethical issues

When asked specific questions about ethical issues within the placement, both trainees were at a loss. This would seem to be related to a possible confusion about the meaning of the term, rather than an absence of thinking. When prompted, **A** began to talk of the difficulty of sharing information in one setting with staff in another. She also spoke of ethical issues in relation to labelling people with psychiatric diagnoses. A distinction was made between ethical issues and ethical procedures.

The message inherent in this feedback is that trainers, supervisors and trainees may benefit from specific thinking in relation to ethics, rather than subsuming this under more general headings. This is of particular concern given that most systemic practitioners are bound by codes of ethics.

The supervisory process and its impact

1. The family

How families were introduced to the setting was obviously important. In both groups, the trainee family therapists were given responsibility for introducing themselves, the setting, the equipment and the team behind the screen. A well-rehearsed format helped both trainees in successfully mastering this task. Although some thought was given to the question of exposing families to the reality of the training context, it was felt, on balance, to be more helpful, by way of introduction, to build on the trainee's existing qualifications and experience. Nevertheless, **A** admitted that at times Down was variously described as her supervisor, or a family therapist who, with other members of the team, would be observing the session from behind the one-way screen. The meanings the family attached to this, and **B**'s use of the earbug during sessions, is open to debate.

Both trainees spoke of their sensitivity in being supervised and the impact of this on the family. For instance, **A** thought that the family would have assumed that she was being told what to do because of the phone-in messages. In other words, someone more senior than her was telling her what to do. She thought that being black would have added to the assumptions the family made about her. Yet, at the same time, when asked how she communicated Down's telephone message to the family, **A** explained that she would usually say 'the team have asked me to ask you'. One possible explanation for this confusion in thinking is that **A**, like many trainees, was acutely aware of the power dynamics operating behind the one-way screen. Although these were not made overt in the actual family sessions, the trainee's sensitivity to being supervised remained alive in her mind and contributed to a feeling of being in a possible one-down position.

2. The team dynamics

Working as part of a team was felt by both trainees to be very helpful in regard to their training needs and in developing a therapeutic style of their own. They both spoke of the value of watching other members of the team working with families and the benefits from the feedback they received when conducting therapy. However, tensions within the team were mentioned, and these were felt to be important in the overall development of the group. For instance, **B**, although sympathetic to differences within the group based on previous learning experiences, still felt that these weakened the systemic focus. In an effort to reinforce the systemic objective, she thought that the supervisor needed to actively intervene in ways that reminded everyone of the purpose of the workshop, rather than respecting differences and trying to work with these.

3. Working practices behind the one-way screen

According to **A**, Down encouraged team members to share their particular interests and, where possible, try to build on these in the workshop. For instance, if a trainee was interested in learning to talk to children, they would be encouraged to observe, during a therapy session, the therapist–child interaction. By and large, Down structured the observing team so that each trainee had a clear task relating to the session and their own learning needs.

Both supervisors, early in their training role, established, first, the means by which they would supervise the trainee therapist in the room and, second, the expectations of those observing the work from behind the one-way screen. **B** had no doubt that McCann was in charge of the therapeutic work. 'An earbug was used for supervision and he was the only one who communicated with the person in the room. Although the observing team were allowed to make suggestions, these may or may not be used in the session or built into the end-of-session message.' Down, on the other hand, did not use an earbug, but instead relied on a telephone link. It was usually agreed beforehand that she would only ring in after the first twenty minutes. The amount of times the supervisors intervened in a session was not specified, although they would, in the end-of-session debriefing, seek to clarify whether, from the trainee's point of view, the interventions were too many or too few. On occasions, the observing teams in both settings were encouraged to reflect in front of the trainee therapist and family in the time-honoured style outlined by Andersen (1990).

Feedback was generally given in the post-session discussions and through video reviews. The issue of trainees playing safe and giving only positive feedback was a feature of both placements. With hindsight, **B** thought that it might be more possible, in line with her development as a family therapist and team member, to risk more constructive criticism. **A**, in regard to this particular point, spoke of a tension in belonging to a group where there were differing levels of training and expertise. She wondered to what extent she had the authority to criticise anyone else's work.

The impact of the supervisor's own training on the trainees

Although both supervisors were in training themselves, trainees for the most part felt protected from the ongoing issues and development of the supervisors, who were training outside their respective therapeutic settings. However, on three occasions, the course consultant (Gorell Barnes) visited the supervisors in their training settings. The purpose of these visits was to observe the supervisors in action, supervising the trainee family therapists. Although **A** and **B** both knew that Gorell Barnes was there to observe the supervisors and not the trainees, they still felt anxious about their practice. For instance, **B** was in the process of applying for a family therapy training and wondered whether Gorell Barnes's observations of her in action might be influential in her securing a place on the course.

There was also some debate as to whether Gorell Barnes had actually stuck to her brief, namely that of supervising the supervisors and not becoming drawn into the clinical work being undertaken by the trainees. **A** thought that Gorell Barnes had, during her visit, failed to resist the pull of the actual therapy. For instance, she offered an alternative perspective on the family work she was observing and did, to some extent, take on a teaching role. **A** was also particularly sensitive to Gorell Barnes offering Down comments about her supervision in front of the trainees. She thought that this may have compromised Down's leadership role, and she would have preferred Gorell Barnes to have tackled Down outside of the therapeutic setting. **B**, on the other hand, valued the comments Gorell Barnes had made about the family work during the inter-session breaks. She also felt that Gorell Barnes was respectful of McCann's position and that his training status did not affect his authority as a supervisor. **B** thought that feedback had been given to McCann outside of the clinical setting. While unaware of the specific feedback, **B** had noticed that McCann adopted a new style after Gorell Barnes's visit. She had been a little confused by the change, noting that McCann shifted from being friendly and social towards them, and instead adopted a more formal and business-like role. He later attributed the change to feedback he had received from Gorell Barnes. However, **B** noted that McCann later reverted to his old style and linked this to her own developmental profile in which the tendency towards cloning trainees gives way to individual ownership and empowerment. Although **A** was unsure of the precise impact of Gorell Barnes's visits on Down's style and performance, she did believe that Down had grown in confidence during the life of the workshop.

Both trainees were asked to comment on the closeness of fit between the supervisor's model of therapy and their own training needs. **B** felt that McCann's model was largely 'post-Milan' (Jones 1993) and linked well with what she was learning on the training offered by the Institute of Family Therapy. **B** also commented on McCann's change in style as she progressed in her work. For instance, at the start of the placement, McCann would give instructions like 'say this' or 'do that', whereas towards the end of the placement, he would suggest **B** explore a particular point. She also pointed out that, as the placement continued, there would be more reflections with the therapist in front of the family. **A** described Down's model as broadly systemic, although she valued her flexible approach in relation to client need.

Learning objectives and outcome

A thought that the main benefit for her in belonging to a training group was the opportunities it afforded in converting theory into practice. She also highlighted the group's potential to generate new ideas that would in turn enrich and expand the therapeutic work with the family. In addition, she thought that her own therapeutic work had developed in response to observing other trainees' therapy sessions with families. For **B**, the training experience had helped her develop particular skills in, for instance, talking to children. She also thought that the family therapy workshop had helped her develop an identity as a systemic practitioner. The extent to which this was subsequently amplified by the direct therapeutic work that took place on the masters training itself was more discontinuous, although it is likely that the development of a systemic identity was helped by both training experiences. Having said this, more thought could have been given to the links between supervised practice in two settings, i.e. one in the community and one that followed in a training agency.

Both trainees particularly valued videotape review and liked the emphases in both placements on 'the self of the therapist'. They thought that the preparation for family meetings was time well spent. Nevertheless, mention was made of the high level of anxiety felt by them when in the room with the family, especially given the 'audience' behind the one-way screen. It would therefore appear that one of the essential ingredients in a training team – namely, the learning that comes from observing others at work, is at the same time – one of the most daunting aspects of the training experience, particularly when it comes to being watched.

References

Andersen, T. (1990) *The Reflecting Team: Dialogues and Dialogues about the Dialogues.* Broadstairs, Kent: Borgmann.

Carroll, M. (1996) *Counselling Supervision. Theory, Skills and Practice.* London: Cassell.

Feltham, C. and Dryden, W. (1994) *Developing Counsellor Supervision.* London: Sage.

Jones, E. (1993) *Family Systems Therapy: Developments in the Milan-Systemic Therapies.* Chichester: Wiley and Sons.

6

Supervision in a Multicultural Context

Gwynneth Down

Feminist critiques have, over the last 10 to 15 years, enabled the family therapy world to rethink their position on gendered power inequalities (previously masked by an emphasis on circularity). The value systems underpinning the therapy and practice of therapy, formerly seen as value-free, have now been exposed, and 'gender issues' are routinely included in both therapy and training.

From this position it has now become possible for the family therapy world to become aware of other power inequalities in society, and to examine systemic models for further value biases.

One such area under scrutiny is in the field of ethnicity and culture. Family therapy models and premises have been developed within particular (largely white/Western) contexts and need to be examined for their appropriateness for working with people across other cultures (Fernando 1991, 1995). As in the field of gender relationships, power differences between peoples of different colour and ethnicity will influence the process of training and therapy. Supervisors and trainers need to attend to these embedded power differences carefully. This chapter will address some of the questions and dilemmas that can arise for supervisors and offer some suggestions for moving forward.

Power and difference in the supervision context

Power inequalities are structured into our society, based on difference. These inequalities are represented in wider systems (for example, in the comparative numbers of women or people from ethnic minority groups in vulnerable positions in the mental health system, or criminal justice system, in distinction from the number in positions of power). However, differences will also be represented in smaller isomorphic episodes such as who speaks, interrupts and listens the most in conversation, and how this differs across genders or within the same gender, or between groups of different ethnicity.

Therapy will be one of the areas where institutional structures of racism may be mirrored in the clinical situation. For example, there are few supervisors or therapists from black or other ethnic minority groups, although these groups may be over-represented in (adult) mental health settings as clients. Littlewood (1992) describes the situation of a white client being seen by a black therapist as a 'status contradiction' (p.11). While the client is seeking help and therefore may be seen to be in a less powerful position, the therapist can be seen as from a disadvantaged group 'from whose position in the social system the white client may already gain economic and status advantages outside the therapy'.

Ethnicity/colour will also be a lens through which black clients view work with a black therapist. While families may initially feel more comfortable knowing that the therapist may understand their position, they may also be suspicious of the therapist being part of the 'white establishment', or see the therapist as second rate (in a form of their own internalised racism; see Boyd-Franklin 1989). There are also the dangers of hoping that a black therapist may be a key to a far larger number of issues than the therapist sees as their domain. In addition, the nuances of 'blackness' in a black worker may be critiqued more heavily by a black client. Such processes may equally apply to the supervision context.

The small number of black supervisors/trainers in the family therapy field will mean that most black trainees do not have role models or mentors who may have more understanding of students' experiences of oppression through their own subjective experience. It is very important that racism is not seen as a 'problem' particular to black peoples and that white supervisors/trainers take responsibility in this area. However, the absence of black trainers/supervisors makes attention to racism in the literature somewhat token and applied only to 'others' (clients), not to ourselves. Training institutions, and those who work in them, need to attend closely to processes that would encourage or discourage black workers from taking up and continuing training. More attention could be paid to grounding trainees' experience through the use of differently positioned caucus groups; for example, for 'black women, black men, black mental health professionals', and in addition 'mentor' systems could be established with black professionals working in the same discipline as a trainee, independent of their family therapy experience.

This author starts from the premise that racism in society has to be seen as the overarching context for relationships between members of different ethnic groups. The trainer/supervisor needs to be aware of the danger of training out 'culture', and of their own racism, stereotyping and prejudice. They need also to be aware of the effect of these dimensions on their practice and how this may affect the work (and lives) of trainees. A point made by Elsa Jones (1990) should also be noted: that while white workers may try not to take part in racist or oppressive practice, we will nonetheless benefit from the more privileged position that we hold in society by virtue of being white and from the dominant culture.

In the context of training and supervision, racism can be externalised and examined to look at the influence that it has on the lives of families, therapists and supervisors. In turn, we can then see what influence we have on the life of racism. What practices do we have that feed and nurture racist practice, however quietly or covertly? What practices do we have that combat racism as it affects what we say or do, or that help and acknowledge the effects on others? As trainers or supervisors, how do we help trainees become aware of how racism may affect them and how racism may influence the relationship between therapist and supervisor?

Cultural issues in family therapy literature

Historically, culture was described in the family therapy literature as something that 'other' families have, families who were not from the white Western norm (or white norm). The culture or ethnicity of either therapist or client was often only mentioned in connection with people not fitting within this group.

This viewpoint can be seen to fit easily with a first-order cybernetics position where the therapist is an outside 'expert' observer to the family. The person of the therapist, their culture, ethnicity or value system were given little thought or prominence. Thus, as in the sexist and gender-blind assumptions of earlier work, family therapy models and techniques have historically often been seen as universal in application, and without cultural bias, in that formative tests in family therapy such as *Families of the Slums* (Minuchin *et al.* 1967) were written by Latino American therapists about Latino culture in the US. Little translation was done in thinking about appropriate adaptations to a UK population.

Indeed, this position may not yet be in the past. Only in 1994, Friedman (described by Falicov 1995) has questioned the need to be sensitive to contextual processes such as race, gender and ethnicity, reasoning that they may not be relevant to basic processes that 'all emotional systems have in common with all protoplasm since creation'. As Falicov (1995) in a US culture and Gorell Barnes (1998) in a UK culture have argued, however, assumptions of what we all have in common will be based on local knowledge itself, grounded in the specific culture in which the view was formulated.

Processes of change towards using second-order cybernetic positions in family therapy (clearly placing the therapist in the 'system'; see Chapter 1) have enabled therapists to review their own value systems and those of their theoretical models.

In tandem with, or perhaps as part of, this process, a number of attempts were made in the 1980s to address difference, by focusing on the particular beliefs, customs or religion associated with a specific ethnic group. Therapists were encouraged to become familiar (if not expert) with the particular culture of the groups with which they were working; for example, the Irish or Hispanic family (e.g. McGoldrick, Pearce and Giordano 1982). While this position has been extremely helpful in exposing the need for cultural sensitivity, it holds all the dangers of stereotyping, and does not acknowledge the huge variations (associated with class, religion, gender, geographical region, etc.) within groups.

In addition, while the given culture(s) will have a profound effect on the way that individuals behave, think, feel, and on what they value, Krause warns against seeing culture as a monolithic 'given' that dictates to the individual, suggesting instead that individuals are active participants 'in reproducing, reconstituting and changing their own cultural contexts' (Krause 1995, p.365).

More recently, the constructivist position has encouraged therapists to think about an individual's personal construction of their situation. From this viewpoint, the term 'culture' has been used to describe the internal beliefs of each particular family (the family culture) rather than to the connection between the family and broader sociocultural context.

In order to be clear about the viewpoint that this author is taking, I will use the definition forwarded by Falicov (1995), who suggested the following multi-dimensional definition of culture:

> ...those sets of shared meanings and adaptive behaviours derived from simultaneous membership and participation in a multiplicity of contexts, such as rural, urban or suburban setting: language, age, gender, cohort, family configuration, race, ethnicity, religion, nationality, socio-economic status, employment, education, occupation, sexual orientation, political ideology; migration and stage of acculturation. (p.375)

This definition expresses some of the complexity of the notion of culture, where wider themes give meaning according to the particular context in which people are operating. It would currently fall under the heading of a social constructionist position.

Culture, families and therapy

This section of the chapter will highlight some areas for consideration in cross-cultural therapy, and is intended as a brief introduction only, to facilitate discussion of the supervision context. It will not aim to fully review the burgeoning literature around these topics.

Much emphasis is given in post-modern family therapy to meaning within social context. It is important to consider, then, the meaning given to the whole process of therapy across cultures. The problem definition(s) by client and therapist, the ideas about the roles and relationship between client and therapist, the therapeutic setting, the conceptualisations of methods of healing, and outcomes may be different between two people from the same broad culture but different region or class. Conceptualisations of these dimensions may be more varied still in cross-cultural work.

It is clear that some conditions now seen as problematic within Western cultures did not 'exist' historically (e.g. ADHD, bulimia), and that cross-culturally the same condition may be perceived either as distress or as one to be taken for granted (Csordas and Kleenman 1990). Problem definition/conceptualisation is clearly important as the indicator for which services may be appropriate and what type of intervention is sought.

Case example

A 14-year-old boy was referred by his GP for severe anxiety symptoms and depression following the death of the paternal grandfather. His parents had emigrated to England from Pakistan 15 to 20 years ago and the grandfather had also come to live with them after their marriage.

While the GP clearly conceptualised the presenting problem as psychiatric, or at least psychological, the boy had a different view. He located his anxiety around his belief or fear that there was no God and his questions about what would happen to his grandfather's soul if this were the case. His grandfather had been a devout Muslim. The family's religious advisers saw the current situation as a crisis of faith and were helping him to pray about this. The boy's parents (who saw themselves as less religious than their son) were unsure about the problem, vacillating between the two ideas and with their own concern that in being too caught up in their own grief, they had failed to help their son with his. The family were seen by a family therapist who clearly could hold many different hypotheses about the meaning of the crisis, in terms of family and wider system dynamics.

Treatment expectations: Clients and therapists

Beliefs about why problems arise and when change is needed to resolve them, and who is needed to make this change happen, have very important implications for the treatment expectations held by clients and therapists, and for the approach that should be chosen for bringing about change. Models of therapy and intervention should properly be seen as 'dominant knowledges' (Foucault 1980) in white/English culture. Systemic, psychoanalytic and medical models developed and used in Western countries become the norms by which people frame their experiences, just as other models or dominant knowledges in non-Western cultures will become explanatory for the same or other experiences. Knowledges that do not fit in with dominant views will become subjugated and may be 'invisible' or seen as 'primitive/exotic'. (For example, in making distinctions between Western and non-Western approaches to healing or therapy, distinction is often made between medical and non-medical types of healing. Non-medical healing in 'other' cultures is often seen as non-scientific, associated with religion and non-professional. It can come as some surprise to find that there are non-Western medical systems such as the ayurvedic medicine of India and Chinese traditional medicines. Non-medical healers can also be defined by sociological definitions as 'professional', and methods of healing can be based on clear empirical assessment processes.)

If therapist and family do not have a good enough 'fit' between their different conceptualisations of problem, treatment and outcome, it is unlikely that their work together will be satisfactory. The family may drop out of treatment, the therapist may feel discouraged and de-skilled and blame the family. How can these issues be addressed in cross-cultural work?

Intercultural matching of therapist/client or supervisor/supervisee is clearly an impossibility in most statutory organisations currently. However, while clear about the great need for more family therapists from black and ethnic minority groups, therapists at the Nafsiyat Intercultural Therapy Centre (Kareem 1992; Thomas 1995) do not advocate intercultural matching of therapist and client. Instead, they suggest that diversity between them can itself be helpful, if the therapist is able to apply an intercultural lens and acknowledge external social disadvantage as real.

As has been mentioned elsewhere in this chapter, the style of therapeutic approach may also be determined by the way a cultural group is organised. Triandis (1994) divides cultures into two types – collectivistic and individualistic. In individualistic cultures the emphasis is on the views, needs and goals of the individual. Individuals are seen as separate from the group and autonomous, and social behaviour is seen as independent from the collective. Collectivistic cultures emphasise cooperative and self-sacrificing behaviour to forward and share the views, needs and goals of the collective. Emotional attachment is to the collective.

Notions of self and relationship are the stuff of which Western therapies are made, and the cultural premises are essential to consider. The formation of the 'self' is influenced by whether we grow up in a collectivistic or individualistic culture. In the former, the self is seen as interdependent and part of a whole (e.g. the Japanese and other Asian cultures), and in the latter the self is independent (e.g. white mainstream English culture) (Lau 1988, 1994; Tamura and Lau 1992).

Littlewood (1992) suggests that family therapy has been shown to be helpful in work with minority or disadvantaged groups in the US (Minuchin 1972) because it attends to a family's shared values rather than notions of individual development. He goes so far as to suggest that 'it now seems likely that it is through family therapy in particular that ideas of selfhood and identity, other than those of the white middle class, can most successfully be employed by therapists in facilitating change' (Littlewood 1989, p.10).

Supervision in a multicultural context

While the literature described has shown changes in thinking about racism and cross-cultural therapy, there has also been a progression in training departments, to inclusion of these topics on training programmes. Specific lectures, workshops and assessed work (e.g. interviewing a non-clinical family from a culture different from your own (Gorell Barnes 1998, Ch.2)) have been introduced. The author's experience from one training context (the first year of Institute of Family Therapy or IFT training) is that lessons have been learnt from the early days of trying to put 'gender on the agenda' (Daniel 1988). There has been an attempt to include issues of power and cross-cultural work onto the core of the training programme, rather than marginalising them into separate, focused lectures alone. Trainers (both internal and external) are required to attend to these dimensions within each lecture or training group. A great deal of further work is needed, however.

Family therapy trainers and supervisors need to become more aware of the 'situated knowledge' of our own professional and personal views (Falicov 1995) and to take a curious stance towards ourselves and our practice. Many of the ideas and suggestions made in this chapter for supervisors to develop with supervisees rest upon the ideal that supervisors will be developing/have developed their own thinking in this area.

In the UK, the accreditation process for supervisors is now quite advanced. Training and accreditation courses are increasing in number and developing over different intakes. Cross-cultural therapy/supervision should be included as a dimension on such courses, by being included in experiential exercises and in academic work. Thus, ideas presented in this section will be described for use in the supervisor/supervisee relationships, but could also be adapted for the training of supervisors.

Hierarchy

In family therapy literature, hierarchy has been assumed to be synonymous with power and often with the presence of oppressive power. This supervisor's view is that power is an element in most, if not all, human relationships, which does not have to be always oppressive in form. Attention and acknowledgement is however needed to prevent it from becoming so.

Supervisors are seen (and expected) to be more experienced and more expert than the supervisee, with the process likened to an apprenticeship (Ault-Riche 1988). There may be a requirement for the supervisor to report on the trainee, either to a training body or in the form of a reference, and for the purpose of the supervision there may be contractual or legal implications for the supervisor in terms of the case or management responsibility. Especially early in the supervisee's training, there will be expectations for them to do therapy in the manner suggested by the supervisor. These inherent power differences may be seen to have similarities to those between therapist and client.

Where a supervisor comes from the dominant (white/Western) group and the supervisee from the non-dominant group (typically being black and from an ethic minority group), these dimensions of supervision can mirror the structured inequality in society between the two groups. Where other supervisees are involved and where gender imbalances and other inequalities are also present, this situation can become more complex.

There has been a general move within the family therapy field to both acknowledge and try to lessen the hierarchy between therapist and client and between supervisor and supervisee. This change has been heralded by feminist-informed practice (which has long had an emphasis on sharing power and information with clients) and post-modern approaches to family therapy.

In considering a feminist-informed supervision process, Wheeler *et al.* (1986) described the importance of 'contracting' to minimise the hierarchy between therapist and supervisor by 'stipulating shared responsibility for learning'. While contracting is frequently used in traditional family therapy training, its use here, to share responsibility for learning as a joint venture, can make the relationship more explicit. The authors also suggest that having a team of supervisees will be effective in lessening the hierarchy. The team will generate multiple views about the same topic, offering a wide range of experiences, which itself can illustrate cultural relativity. The supervisor should encourage each supervisee to give their views, and show that difference is valued, rather than try to dissolve or negotiate away difference.

Post-modern approaches place emphasis on therapeutic discourse or conversation as the medium by which learning and change take place. Replacing the first-order cybernetic expert 'outside' position, it is now acknowledged that the 'Knower' is situated in particular contexts and times, and 'knowledge' itself is socially constructed through language.

Using this framework, Anderson and Swim (1995) suggest that the role of a supervisor is as more of a mentor than an expert, having expertise in exploratory conversational process, but not being an expert on the supervisee. The supervisee is the expert on his/her own life, narratives, experiences and knowledge, with the supervisor engaging collaboratively with them 'in telling, enquiring, interpreting and shaping' of the narratives.

While the position of co-construction of meaning can be seen to be helpful in lessening the hierarchy from the supervisor's point of view, Bobele, Gardener and Biever (1995) remind us that there are at least two people involved in defining the relationship. Supervisees (and others) will often view the supervisor as the expert, even if the supervisor wishes to adapt or be seen a different way.

Anderson and Swim (1995) advocate a position of 'not knowing' in supervision, described earlier (by Anderson and Goolishian 1992) in relation to therapy: '...by not knowing we mean a general attitude or stance, that the supervisor does not have access to privileged exclusive information, can never fully understand another person, and always needs to learn more about what has been said or not said' (p.7). The supervisor needs to be aware of the context of their own 'knowledge' and be open to being informed by the supervisee.

The aim of the supervisor then would be to facilitate a process in which the supervisee's ideas and voice are heard in ways which expand the options for thinking about the issues of therapy, and helps the supervisee to develop self-competence and self-agency.

Anti-racist ground rules

In the very early joining stages of a training or supervisory relationship, discussion should take place about the ground rules and contract for working. This can then be reviewed at various stages. Particularly in group situations, early discussion can take place about anti-racist work. The supervisor/trainer can state his/her aims in this area and invite discussion about how this may be achieved. A statement that the supervisor (in particular) and trainees all have responsibility for trying to ensure that the process of learning is anti-oppressive (i.e. in use of language or process) can be made, and trainees then asked how they would like issues to be addressed. An example of trainee or supervisor making a racist comment inadvertently in team discussion could be offered, and thought given as to how this could be dealt with.

While this will often usefully lead to conversations about how to deal with racist comments made by clients, it is important to address the supervisory process first. This can acknowledge that therapists live in a racist context and they may get 'caught out' by racism, while also giving explicit permission for this dimension to be raised.

Kareem (1992) has stated his belief that it is the responsibility of the therapist, from the outset, to address issues of ethnicity and racism with clients. It is equally the supervisor's responsibility to raise these issues with trainees without leaving the onus on them. The way in which the supervisor manages this situation will be helpful for supervisees in thinking about how they will raise these issues with clients.

Supervisor/therapist attitude

The development of a framework that integrates differing cultural viewpoints into the supervisory/therapy situation cannot be achieved by use of particular techniques and exercises alone, although some are described here. Instead, it involves the supervisor in developing a posture 'that develops through awareness of the role that values play for families, for therapists, and for the encounter with each other' (Falicov 1995).

Students and supervisors may be hampered by their ethnocentric view of the world, being ignorant of areas or questions that they are not addressing, because they are simply not aware of other views! This author had barely considered the concept of the 'dominant dyad' or 'primary axis' (Hsu 1972) in family organisation. The emphasis or public value placed on the primary dyadic relationship (e.g. husband–wife, father–son, mother–son) within a cultural group will result in different family systems which will contribute to characteristic thought and behaviour patterns shown by different family members (Hsu 1972). Therapists/supervisors need to be aware that these differences may exist in order to have this probability in their repertoire of thinking.

Elsewhere in this chapter, criticism has been made about ethnic-focused study, where it has been used as the sole component for study of cross-cultural work. In conjunction with other methods and attitudes, however, it can be used to enhance supervisor/supervisee knowledge about areas for comparison and enquiry. Trainers/supervisors can suggest reading (e.g. Hardy and Laszloffy 1994; Tseng and Hsu 1991), perhaps also taking Falicov's four parameters of ecological context, migration and acculturation, family organisation, and family life cycle (outlined further below) as the focus. This could be both non-professional and professional literature.

Social constructionist positions bring many strengths to cross-cultural work. There is emphasis on multiple views and no one absolute reality, on the importance of context at all levels of human experience and relationships, and on co-construction in the therapeutic setting. Thus, a supervisor and therapist using this therapeutic position will be oriented to attend to wider sociocultural contexts, in addition to the particular individual characteristics of a therapist or family. Valuing multiple views may help the supervisor/therapist to attain a culturally relativistic framework for assessment and intervention, and may help them to 'develop an exploratory, sensitive and respectful attitude toward the client's cultural identity' as part of a co-constructed supervision process.

The attitude of 'not knowing' (Anderson and Swim 1995) in post-modern supervision, described earlier, also has many similarities with the idea of 'cultural naïveté' proposed by Dyche and Zayas (1995, p.394). Naïveté is described as a 'sense of openness and receptivity, a condition of unknowing that is without anxiety or self-consciousness'. The supervisor will need to be mindful of their own ethnocentrism and stereotyping to try to adopt an attitude of 'interest and sociological imagination' (Wright Mills 1959) and 'respectful curiosity' (Cecchin 1987) in their supervision.

Falicov (1995) cites research which suggests that those who pay less attention to cultural issues, particularly when in positions of power, are more likely to stereotype others (Fiske 1993). In order to counter this, the supervisor must try to develop genuine interest in their trainees' cultural beliefs and constraints, rather than following their own assumptions and precepts. In adopting this attitude, the supervisor is both trying to model for the supervisees a way in which they might work respectfully with people from different cultures from their own and helping them to become aware of their own 'cultural baggage'.

The process of supervision will be a reciprocal learning exercise where both supervisor and supervisees learn which questions/lines of enquiry seem useful and in which circumstances. Both supervisor and supervisees will learn when overt links with cultural themes are useful to the process of supervision or therapy and when this does not seem directly relevant to the 'here and now'.

Re-acculturating the mind

Falicov (1988) suggested that training/supervision needs to enable trainees to develop 'multidimensional comparative frameworks' for cross-cultural work. In a more recent paper (Falicov 1995), she has developed this idea further by proposing four key parameters for comparison – ecological context, migration and acculturation, family organisation and family life cycle. The developing use of these comparative parameters for thinking how a family and their social context may be positioned within any culture should fit alongside the development of 'respectful curiosity' (Cecchin 1987) and 'cultural naïveté' (Dyche and Zayas 1995) to shape therapist's attitude and enquiry (as described above).

The use of comparative parameters can be used to understand the cultural maps that a therapist brings, and then to look at the consonance and dissonance between the family, therapist and supervisor's maps. As in other areas of therapy, it is important that there is a good enough 'fit' between the three levels. In the complex area of live supervision, however, it can be seen that there may be areas of similarity or difference that are too close. Trying to find connections or areas that promote curiosity may be helpful in joining with therapist or family. Bridges of cultural connectedness can become apparent, and interest in each other's world views and experiences can forge new understanding and respect where differences occur.

In a supervision group, this process can also be explored, with supervisees discussing these dimensions amongst themselves and discovering experientially their importance and usefulness.

Supervisees could be asked to consider and develop questions that they might ask of each other about these parameters and to have the opportunity to ask and compare answers within the group. While this process may be most helpful between supervisees of differing cultural backgrounds, 'same group' supervisees may be helped to discover similarity and difference based on social class, religion or region within the group. It may be discovered which questions elicited new ways of thinking, which seemed respectful/disrespectful and which provided access to cultural beliefs or values for questioner and questioned. Krause (1995) has illustrated that some aspects of culture may not be easily accessed by direct questioning, and this difficulty will become apparent in the discussion. Supervisees might be asked to think of symbols that might express aspects of their culture, where words are more difficult.

Where supervisees and/or supervisor come from different cultural backgrounds, one exercise with both serious and potentially amusing application is for supervisor and supervisees to consider what experiences might help others (or themselves) to be more aware of their culture. Raval (1993) described the following examples:

- Supervisor and trainee to sample ethnic cuisine (e.g. go to English restaurant).

- Supervisor and trainee to take part in local practices (e.g. take part in a fight at a football match).

- Supervisor and trainee to learn a new language or dialect (e.g. Cockney).

- Supervisor and trainee to understand a new religious practice (e.g. worship of dogs at betting shop).

When trainees have had the opportunity for considering these dimensions with each other, they may then be more readily able to transfer their thinking and questions to the therapeutic context. The supervisor can facilitate the process of hypothesising and generating appropriate areas for questions, which connect with the issues that the family bring to therapy.

The cultural genogram

The 'ethnic-focused' approach to cross-cultural training has been criticised earlier for the inherent dangers of stereotyping groups (Falicov 1995). The increasing number of ethnic and cultural groups, as well as the increase in mixed ethnic families with multicultural practices, who will be seen in clinical practice also mitigates against the possibility of becoming knowledgeable about all cultures, even were this a relevant aim. A more relevant aim would be to help trainees to become culturally competent and sensitive in a manner which can be generalised to working with peoples from many different cultures.

Many papers describing cross-cultural work propose that trainees need to become aware and have some understanding of their own culture before being able to understand others. Holland (1992) suggested that most ideas about culture are held abstractly, and only when they become salient to personal circumstances do they become activated. It is therefore important that this understanding is not only at a cognitive level, but also connects on an emotional, personal level.

The genogram has been widely used as a training tool, often to help trainees to get in touch with their family of origin issues, and how these may impact on their work with client families (Bahr 1990). It can be used in supervision groups for recognising the different life experiences that the training group represents and the 'lenses' through which trainees may view the work.

Hardy and Laszloffy (1995) have added another dimension to the use of genograms – the cultural genogram, the primary goal of which is 'to promote cultural awareness and sensitivity by helping trainees to understand their cultural identities' (p.228). Trainees are helped to gain further insight into, and appreciation for, the ways in which culture affects their role as therapists and influences the life of clients in treatment.

Attention should be given to timing in use of the cultural genogram. Discussing both personal information and dimensions of culture and ethnicity can be very powerful, and can give rise to strong feelings which need to be dealt with by the supervisor and trainees. Thus, the cultural genogram should not be used too early in the supervision group's life together. (However, the authors' experience is that the cultural genograms can also be helpful in building relationships and lessening hierarchy, particularly if the supervisor is prepared to share aspects of their own cultural genogram.) As in the use of genograms with clients, at least one further session will be needed to deal with the process, although it is likely that issues will continue to be raised throughout the life of the group.

Supervisees should be asked to prepare their own cultural genogram before-hand – drawing their own genogram, and choosing colours to represent cultural groups (e.g. filling in genogram symbols with appropriate colours including mixes). Symbols can also be created to 'express the intuitive and affective aspects of cultural issues which are sometimes difficult to capture with words' (Hardy and Laszloffy 1995, p.228).

Hardy and Laszloffy suggest a series of questions for supervisees to consider while preparing the genogram and for the supervisor/facilitator during discussion of the genogram. These will need to be adapted (as the language is American). Indeed, if time permitted, trainees could be encouraged to devise their own questions.

The cultural genogram can be a very potent tool for helping supervisees to consider their own culture. In a group setting, supervisees will have the experience of cultural relativism at first hand, as they each have different responses and ideas to the same questions. Being able to see areas of difference and similarity, both from someone within the same broad cultural group and from outside of it, will help trainees find new ways of connecting with each other about cultural issues.

It can be seen that the process of making a cultural genogram and following themes through questions may be excellent training for trainees in talking with clients about aspects of family and culture. The role of supervisor in supporting this process is also isomorphic with the process. He/she needs to ensure that the process is safe enough and yet offers the possibility of challenge and new information for supervisees (and indeed supervisor).

Conclusion

Clearly, there is a need for new approaches to therapy and supervision in order to provide ethical and effective services across cultures. However, enthusiasm for this work has to be tempered if not to miss the point. Rather than interest only in culture to the exclusion of all else, it is clear that other important factors may be important for the family (e.g. poverty) at this time. Questions around culture may be fascinating for therapist/supervisor, but they must be linked to the purpose of the meeting to help to resolve some problem or complaint: they should seem appropriate to the family. Asking clients 'is this something that is important to you?' will be one way of checking this out.

In summary, this chapter has attempted to look at some of the dimensions of cross-cultural therapy and supervision. There has been an emphasis on the need for supervisors to become aware of their own cultural biases and to become open to new ways of thinking prior to helping supervisees to do the same. This cross-cultural awareness needs to be developed in both cognitive and experiential 'feeling' dimensions, and exercises have been described that might begin to address these. Following Dyche and Zayas (1995), I have suggested that the use of the positions of 'respectful curiosity' and 'cultural naïveté' by the supervisor with the supervisees will be isomorphic with an appropriate stance for therapists in cross-cultural therapy.

The effects of racism on the supervision process at all levels has been discussed, and the special responsibilities of the supervisor in addressing these have been laid out. Family therapy has been through periods of rapid change in the last 10 to 20 years. The development of cross-cultural therapy and appropriate supervision for this is one current growth area which provides exciting challenges to the field and will ultimately make the field more effective for all clients.

References

Anderson, H. and Goolishian, H. (1992) 'The client is the expert: A not knowing approach to therapy.' In S. McNamee and K. Gergen (eds) *Constructing Therapy: Social Construction and the Therapeutic Process.* London: Sage Publications.

Anderson, H. and Swim, S. (1995) 'Supervision as collaborative conversation: Connecting the voices of supervisor and supervisee.' *Journal of Systemic Therapies 14,* 2, 1–13.

Ault-Riche, M. (1988) 'Teaching an integrated model of family therapy: Women as students, women as supervisors.' In L. Braverman (ed) *Women, Feminism and Family Therapy.* New York: Haworth Press.

Bahr, K. (1990) 'Student responses to genogram and family chronology.' *Journal of Family Relations 39,* 3, 243–249.

Bobele, M., Gardener, G. and Biever, J. (1995) 'Supervision as social construction.' *Journal of Systemic Therapies 14,* 2, 14–25.

Boyd-Franklin, N. (1989) *Black Families in Therapy.* New York: Guildford Press.

Cecchin, G. (1987) 'Hypothesising, circularity and neutrality revisited: An invitation to curiosity.' *Family Process 26,* 405–413.

Csordas, T. and Kleinman, A. (1990) 'The therapeutic process.' In T. Johnson and C. Sargent (eds) *Medical Anthropology: A Handbook of Theory and Method.* New York and London: Greenwood Press.

Daniel, G. (1988) Personal Communication. *Putting Gender on the Agenda.* Lecture for first-year introductory course at IFT.

Dyche, L. and Zayas, L.H. (1995) 'The value of curiosity and naïveté for the cross-cultural psychotherapist.' *Family Process 34,* 4, 389–401.

Falicov, C. (1995) 'Training to think culturally: A multidimensional comparative framework.' *Family Process 34,* 4, 373–389.

Fernando, S. (1991) *Mental Health, Race and Culture.* London: Macmillan/MIND.

Fernando, S. (1995) *Mental Health in a Multi-Ethnic Society: A Multidisciplinary Handbook.* London and New York: Routledge.

Fiske, S. (1993) 'Controlling other people: The impact of power on stereotyping.' *American Psychologist 48,* 6, 621–628.

Foucault, M. (1980) *Power/Knowledge; Selected Interviews and Other Writings.* New York: Pantheon.

Friedman (1994) 'Sensitivity to contextual variables: A legitimate learning objective for all supervisors?' *The Supervision Bulletin* 7, 2, 4–7.

Gorell Barnes, G. (1998) *Family Therapy in Changing Times.* Basingstoke: Macmillan.

Hardy, K. and Laszloffy, T. (1994) 'Deconstructing place in family therapy.' *Journal of Feminist Family Therapy 3*, 4, 5–33.

Hardy, K. and Laszloffy, T. (1995) 'The cultural genogram: Key to training culturally competent family therapists.' *Journal of Marital and Family Therapy 12*, 3.

Holland, D. (1992) 'How cultural systems become desire: A case study of American romance.' In R. D'Andrade and C. Strauss (eds) *Human Motives and Cultural Models.* Cambridge: Cambridge University Press.

Hsu, F.L.K. (1972) 'Kinship and ways of life: An exploration.' In F.L.K. Hsu (ed) *Psychological Anthropology.* Cambridge: Schenkman.

Jones, E. (1990) 'Feminism and family therapy: Can mixed marriages work?' In R.J. Perelberg and A. Miller (eds) *Gender and Power in Families.* London: Tavistock/Routledge.

Kareem, J. (1992) 'The Nafsiyat Intercultural Therapy Centre: Ideas and experience in intercultural therapy.' In J. Kareem and R. Littlewood *Intercultural Therapy: Themes Interpretations and Practice.* London: Blackwell Scientific Publications.

Krause, I.B. (1995) 'Personhood, culture and family therapy.' *Journal of Family Therapy 17*, 4, 363–383.

Lau, A. (1988) 'Family therapy and ethnic minorities.' In E. Street and W. Dryden (eds) *Family Therapy in Britain.* Milton Keynes and Philadelphia: Open University Press.

Lau, A. (1994) 'Gender, culture and family life.' In G. Gorell Barnes (ed) *Ethnicity, Culture, Race and Family Therapy.* Family Therapy, Context 20. Canterbury: AFT Publishing.

Littlewood, R. (1989) 'Glossary.' In Report of the Royal College of Psychiatrist Special (Ethnic Issues) Committee. London: Royal College of Psychiatrists.

Littlewood, R. (1992) 'Towards an intercultural therapy.' In J. Kareem and R. Littlewood *Intercultural Therapy. Themes, Interpretations and Practice.* London: Blackwell Scientific Publications.

McGoldrick, M., Pearce, J.K. and Giordano, J. (eds) (1982) *Ethnicity and Family Therapy.* New York: Guildford Press.

Minuchin, S. and Minuchin, P. (1974) *Families and Family Therapy.* Cambridge: Harvard University Press.

Minuchin, S., Montalvo, B., Guerney, J.R., Rosman, B.L. and Schumer, F. (1967) *Families of the Slums.* New York and London: Basic Books.

Raval, H. (1993) 'Thoughts on teaching and supervision.' From notes on Race and Culture Training in Clinical Psychology, University of East London. (unpublished, with permission of author).

Tamura, T. and Lau, A. (1992) 'Connectedness and separateness: Applicability of family therapy and Japanese families.' *Family Process 31*, 4, 319–340.

Thomas, L. (1995) 'Psychotherapy in the context of race and culture: An intercultural therapeutic approach.' In S. Fernando (ed) *Mental Health in a Multicultural Society: A Multidisciplinary Handbook*. London: Routledge.

Triandis, H.C. (1994) 'Major cultural syndromes and emotions.' In S. Kitayama and H.R. Markus (eds) *Emotion and Culture: Empirical Studies of Mutual Influence*. Washington DC: American Psychological Association.

Tseng, W. and Hsu, J. (1991) *Culture and Family: Problems and Therapy*. New York: The Haworth Press.

Wheeler, *et al.* (1985) 'Rethinking family therapy education and supervision: A feminist model.' *Journal of Psychiatry and the Family* 53–71.

Wright Mills, C. (1959) *The Sociological Imagination*. London: Oxford University Press.

7

Gender and Systemic Supervision

Gwynneth Down, Gill Gorell Barnes and Damian McCann

As long as the world is an unfair place, as long as patriarchy prevails, love will be tainted by domination, subordination will be eroticized to make it tolerable and symptoms will be necessary to keep families from flying apart. (Goldner 1988, p.30)

These powerful words mark a point in the development of family therapy when feminism was creating an alternative series of discourses about men, women and family life and theories about change, from which the systemic field could be assessed and critiqued. Feminist theorising offered an ongoing provocation to any theoretical approach which claimed it could offer a complete model for understanding and treating family problems in context. From the mid-1970s it offered an emotional and intellectual lens through which to explore the assumptive base of systemic practice, although the impact feminism offered in the family therapy field in the UK did not begin to be felt until the mid-1980s.

In writing this chapter we are each aware that we write as part of larger collective. It would not be viable to draft any thoughts relating to supervision, gender and family therapy without drawing on certain key names who have charted the territory over the last 15 years. Some of these are specifically referenced below. However, the larger thinking with which ideas are permeated cannot be individually referenced, and we would like to acknowledge that the chapter stands as a marker with a constantly expanding field, to the field of ideas, rather than as an original starting point.

During the 1970s, women therapists began to develop a collective voice which they identified as having features distinct from the preoccupations of men working alongside them. Many of these preoccupations centred around unacknowledged inequalities in the field itself, both in what was addressed in theory and in training, and what was ignored in practice. In relation to socially structured inequalities specifically affecting women and children, Walters (1990) summarised the early feminist approach as including four major components:

- The conscious inclusion of the different experience of women in their professional, social and family roles in a culture largely organised by male experience.

- A critique of therapy practices which devalued women and their roles.

- The integration of feminist therapy and women's studies into family therapy thinking.

- The use of female modes and models in practice and teaching.

In addition, a feminist approach increasingly argued for an altered consciousness about the realities of power and control in families, especially those aspects of physical and economic control which oppressed and isolated women and children (Jones 1990, 1995). However, differences within feminist thinking – 'feminism's' rather than one overarching voice – themselves developed over two decades. Goldner, in her account of early developments (Goldner 1988), has narrated ways in which the interaction of ideologies from sociology and psychoanalysis in the US impacted on women therapists who were developing their own ways of constructing theory and practice. Legacies from these two parallel dominant discourses emphasised the desirability of an unbalanced hierarchy to be seen as a prerequisite of 'good' family life (Parsons and Bales 1955; Skynner 1976). Goldner describes, for example, how the power of certain contemporary ideologies about the good practices of motherhood, in which 'woman and her subjectivity of voice was subjugated to the provision of a good enough environment for her child', powerfully affected the development of young feminist women therapists at the time:

> ...women never appear as independently existing subjects with their own interiority and personal desires, or if they do, this stance is characterised pejoratively as a pathological abdication of their primary responsibility to submerge their personhood for the good of the family. (Goldner 1991, p.103)

The growth of feminist research and scholarship in the social sciences created much more vivid distinctions that needed to be taken into account when attending to women-led households and the position of women as carers in families (Walters 1990). The feminisation of poverty as a major issue for social researchers in the UK in the 1980s provided a parallel alternative discourse about the realities of family life, inviting attention to differentials of economic and socially constructed power that went alongside those of physical and sexual isolation and abuse (Gorell Barnes 1994; Jones 1991).

Just as gender difference and power inequalities became recognised as dimensions of family life which were being assumed as 'normal', it was also recognised that some aspects of training relationships, including techniques and inter-ventions which were taught, actively disadvantaged women. 'Male-derived, male-focused ideas about behaviour and relationships' were an integral part of early family therapy training, theory and practice (Weiner and Boss 1985), and stereotypic gender-role behaviour and dominant, male-led hierarchies had been reinforced in training institutions (Caust, Libow and Ruskin 1981). Both men and women were constricted in their ability to experiment with and adopt alternative modes of behaviour in the supervision and therapy context.

Undertaking training in the 1980s (as Down and McCann did) meant joining a changing field. There was great uncertainty about the possibility of integrating gender critiques into systemic theory and practice. The process of promoting what amounted to second-order change in the field was by no means straight-forward. Debate was often heated and polarised into an either/or position.

Using feminist arguments about power was seen by some as linear, unsystemic and 'political' (current theory being seen as 'neutral' or 'apolitical'), while some feminist critics viewed systems theory as a lightly veiled attempt to 'blame the victims' (women and children) and maintain a patriarchal status quo. Family therapists who had earlier accused individual therapists of failing to consider the (family) context in which their clients lived had fallen into the same trap – ignoring the wider social political context for family life and for their own theories and practice. Without an ability to consider these contexts, it did not then seem possible to adopt a both/and position in relation to reciprocity and power in relationships.

However, some of the UK trainers and supervisors of that time were at the forefront of examining theory and practice using gendered lenses (Charlotte Burck, Gwyn Daniels, Elsa Jones), and thus trainees of that time were provided with both a context and language for considering aspects of the field that had previously been 'invisible' (Walters et al. 1988).

The intense emotions, argument and 'resistance to change' that characterised reactions to early feminist critiques to the field may now be more associated with the discussions around 'race' and culture that are beginning to take place. It is questionable, however, whether the impetus for change in the area of gender (provided largely by female therapists) will be mirrored in the process of developing 'racial' and cultural awareness – will our predominantly white Western field take on the challenge of deconstructing the dominance of white Western cultural premises on our work or will lip-service only be paid?

For women who came to a feminist position in their 40s rather than their 20s, such as one of these authors (Gorell Barnes), the reconstruction of their own journey as therapists, trainers and supervisors in the 1970s and 1980s included a developing recognition of the degree to which their thinking had been shaped by constant adaptation to the requirements of a male-organised society, what Jones

(1995) has named *andocracy* rather than *patriarchy*. For Gorell Barnes this also included a higher education context in which the capacity of women to think was itself regarded as suspect by many of her fellow students, a tension continuing into early professional life and training.

Winnicott, a psychoanalyst who taught at the time of Gorell Barnes's own mental health training, wrote about the 'true and false self' (in relation primarily as his texts show to women clients) in ways which may be relevant to requote here for women in the new millennium thinking about themselves as trainers and supervisors in the future. Winnicott described the development of a 'false self' (a social self) which exists to defend the 'true self', which may be hidden away but is acknowledged as having potential and being allowed a secret life. He related these layers of 'hiding' to depression in women: '…here is the clearest example of clinical illness as an organization with a positive aim, the preservation of the individual in spite of abnormal environmental conditions' (Winnicott 1960, p.143). Re-analysing this in a piece of work that took place during the 1980s, Gorell Barnes reformulated this for herself in terms of critiquing the dichotomy of true and false self : '…perhaps it is more useful to consider aspects of one's own being, or potential, that are brought forth in particular contexts in ways that are functional at the time' (Gorell Barnes and Henesy 1994, p.83). For young girls this used to include socially-prescribed ideas about compliance, especially to older men and women. For Gorell Barnes as therapist and theorist, this led to a different route for critiquing practice. Instead of openly confronting older male teachers who privileged certain kinds of male-led family structure above others, through an informed and strong feminist voice, which she lacked; she struggled to clarify research-related bases for systemic thinking in relation to different models of family living. She then offered critiques of theory and dominant, male-led discourses from a more empirical knowledge base. The importance of exploring differences in thoughts and attitudes, pathways into therapy and gendered positions available in a supervision group, has been accentuated by the research into gendered development and differential thinking. Such writings show that, from many different orientations, the deconstruction of gender and gendered premises can be central to freeing men and women for creative thinking (Gilligan 1982; Gorell Barnes 1996; Haste 1987; Lloyd 1987; Maccoby 1988; Steadman 1985).

Training and supervision have essential contributions to make in providing contexts where closed aspects of the gendered self of both clients and therapists can be explored in relative safety.

Style and practice

Jones, in her retrospective paper on the construction of gender in society and family therapy (1995), gives a powerful analysis of the wider social forces shaping and privileging certain characteristics of discourse, both within wider society and within the therapy domain. Goldner (1991) asserted that the emphasis on logical debate and reasoning favoured by male practitioners had silenced many female trainees and practitioners who did not wish to think and act in ways that felt dystonic. These women attempted to find alternative, 'personal, self-disclosing and self-observing stances' in both therapy and research. Goldner believes that this temporarily led to a dread of taking up aspects of what had become equated with masculinity and compromised the feminist movement in the US, by silencing through depriving them of the pleasure associated with argument and theory building. However, in Europe at least, models of therapy themselves were in flux during the 1980s. The inclusion of women's talk as part of therapy training and supervision contributed in ways that interacted with a post-Milan approach, which focused on the use of words and questions, rather than action and directives, and the rise of interest in constructivist and social constructionist positions within the systemic field (Burck and Daniel 1994; Gorell Barnes 1998; Jones 1993). Each contributed to recognising plurality of experience and the importance of including subjectivity in the interpersonal experience of therapy. These changes reflected those taking place in the world outside – a world that is (arguably) more accepting of difference between people – in sexuality, culture, ethnicity, class and gender – and that has begun to acknowledge the power imbalances that accompany those differences.

In the European field in the 1980s, a preoccupation with finding a 'woman's voice' (in distinction from a male voice), which had characterised the early impact that feminist women thinkers brought to family therapy, was overlaid by recognising the importance of distinctions between the experiences of men, of women, of different ethnicities, of different economic status, of different age (MacKinnon and Miller 1987; Speed 1991). Harding (1987) in considering class, race and gendered identity, has put it thus:

> Once it is realized that there is not universal man, but only culturally different men and women, then man's eternal companion, woman, also disappeared. That is women come only in different classes, races, and cultures, there is no 'woman' and no 'woman's experience'. (p.6)

Gender, difference and training

Hare-Mustin and Maracek (1990) have described how the field of psychological theory and research attended to the study of gender and gendered relationships in the 20th century within the US. Like Goldner and Jones, they delineate how mankind was used to represent humankind in many different spheres, and women were largely absent either as investigators or as objects of inquiry. Male-experienced behaviour and development were generalised into universal truths about both men and women. The profound effects of this in the 1970s was shown in Broverman *et al*.'s study of mental health professionals within the US, in which male-gendered behaviour was defined as normal and desirable, whereas female-gendered behaviour was defined as proof of mental ill health, although also being defined as normative for females (Broverman *et al*. 1970).

However, as the field began to take note of gender difference, a dichotomy between men and women and ideas of femininity and masculinity was continually presented. Although it may seem bizarre to quote a theory from the 1950s as illustrative of the attitudes characterising the development of roles both in family life and theory about family life, and the relationship of that theory to training developments, Parson's gender-role theory, which dominated social theories in the 1950s and 1960s, suggested that men were instrumental and task oriented while women were expressive and oriented towards relationships and behaviours. This stereotype persisted in the theorising about family structure and functioning (Minuchin and Minuchin 1974) and therefore how to address it up until the middle 1980s.

In that context, it was argued that early family therapy models privileged the use of assertive, instrumental behaviours by therapists rather than relational expressive behaviours. Structural and strategic therapies in particular required therapists to tackle a more active, orchestrative stance, usually seen as part of stereotypical male behaviour (Haley 1985; Minuchin and Minuchin 1974). Many women felt actively uncomfortable in using some of the behaviours advocated in this body of techniques, although others used them with their own adaptations of understanding of family organisation in female-headed families (Walters *et al*. 1988) or modified 'directiveness' through the use of more playful techniques (Madanes 1981). Caust, Libow and Ruskin (1981), however, suggested that structural and strategic models offered female therapists 'opportunities' to break away from the stereotyped, nurturant, reactive skills and encourage the trainee to begin experiencing herself as an instrumental, rather than solely expressive, change agent.

Within these suggestions, however, lay hidden values that women trainees should be able to achieve the same skills and 'be as good as' the men. The lack of recognition of the value of stereotyped feminine attributes such as sensitivity, warmth and empathy was highlighted by research into family therapy trainees' gendered beliefs (about themselves and others). Both men and women described themselves as having more stereotypically male characteristics as they progressed through training (Down 1992). Challenges to stereotypical behaviour and beliefs during training may have placed more emphasis on traditionally feminine traits because of their lower social value and promoted stereotypical masculine attributes.

With the modern emphasis on subjectivity, language and conversational styles, however, it could now be argued that it is men (as clients, therapists, supervisors) who are more at a disadvantage currently:

> The effects of feminist critiques have been witnessed on training courses which give gender a high profile, and when as great an emphasis is placed on personal development as on the acquisition of technical skills or theoretical learning, men sometimes express the view that women are better placed to benefit from training than they are. (Burck and Daniel 1995, p.127)

Burck and Daniel question whether this leads to men taking seriously the need to attend to issues of gender for themselves or whether they are worried about losing a competitive edge in a more 'feminised' field.

Focusing on difference between men and women may hold its own difficulties. Social constructionist and constructivist positions acknowledge that an observer is never wholly separate from the thing observed, and clearly there is no 'objective' view on gender that men and women can take. As in the wider field of psychology, family therapy theory veers between exaggerating gender differences and ignoring or minimising them (described by Hare-Mustin and Maracek (1990) as 'alpha and beta biases' respectively).

Therapists and supervisors need to have a wide range of roles available to them that are based on personal choice and interpersonal negotiation rather than on sex-role prescriptions (Wheeler *et al.* 1986). Gender 'differences' are, of course, culturally specific and historically fluid, not universal or essential. It is important then to avoid the danger of decontextualising – focusing on the individual context, rather than on the wider socio-political context in which the meaning of gender is created. Burck and Daniel (1994, p.7) suggest that three levels need to be held in mind:

- The subjective level of gendered premises for individual men and women.

- The way these premises are brought forth in interaction, i.e. the relational level.

- The societal constraints and opportunities for women and men, and their impact on relationships and individual experience. (p.7)

In bringing gender into supervision, we need to consider how we address the politicised (socially constructed) issues of gender within the supervisory relationship itself, and within the team, as well as between the therapist and the family – how we make the 'sexual politics of observed and observing systems' a subject for therapeutic conversation (Goldner 1991). Love and power need deconstructing within the socially constructed and politicised domains of gender, ethnicity, and class. Jones (1995), considering how a culture constructs and instructs gendered identities, has suggested we need to ask in each (family/supervision) context

> which aspects of human diversity are encouraged and which suppressed? What are they allowed or not allowed to do, encouraged to feel or express, and what not? What are the assumptions regarding maleness and femaleness which the wider culture fosters, and how do these assumptions express themselves in sub-cultures and local social groupings, in families and in the self-characterization of individuals? What are men and women taught about what they may be allowed to get away with? (p.18)

Burck and Daniel (1994) have further challenged family therapists not to resort at any time to gender stereotyping in the use of feminist theorising, but to recognise the contextualisation of gender:

> What is femaleness and maleness? The question implies that somewhere, somehow we could find out what womanhood and manhood is. We take the view that these categories have been created through language, which in turn has real effects on how we live, think, and feel. This is not to deny that there are actual biological differences, but that these are so profoundly mediated through culture that it is impossible to find a gendered essence: we can only discover the ways in which we perform these differences. (p.11)

Addressing complexity

It has already been argued (in Chapter 6) that training about issues of difference and power should be integral to courses rather than being taught as separate sections, not least because compartmentalising can regulate fundamental topics to a theoretical and clinical sideline. Crucially, the complexity of interaction between dimensions of difference ('race', gender, ethnicity, sexuality, culture, disability, class) is also often lost when approaching each as a 'special issue'. We are aware that in producing chapters specifically addressing gender, race and culture, we may be falling into this trap, and thus in this section we wish to discuss examples from the practice of supervision. Supervision, we believe, offers unique opportunities for addressing this complexity.

Case example

A white/European female family therapist offered live consultation to a family therapy training team of three participants within a health service setting. The participants of the group included a Japanese female psychologist, a black/English female social worker and a white/English male psychiatrist. All were at different stages in family therapy training.

The group members had elected to meet for a half-day each week to see clients referred to the service. There was also a verbal contract to attend to group and individual issues in order to develop self-reflexive practice, to highlight the resources that the group had to offer both clients and each other, and to attempt to be aware of possible constraints to their work.

A supervision group can offer different viewpoints and challenges in a way that a single supervisor and trainee cannot. This group represented difference in cultural and ethnic backgrounds, gender, role and class (the latter being frequently overlooked). In the particular work setting, as well as the wider socio-political context, these differences proffer different levels of status and power. The supervisor wanted therefore to ensure that these differences were considered early in the group's life together. She hoped that this would invite the participants to take responsibility for considering their own practice in relation to power difference, but also to give permission for the hierarchy (of which she was a significant figure!) to be discussed. With this in mind, the group had undertaken various exercises. The first of these was to set ground rules (see Chapter 6) by which the group would operate, including explicit exploration of group differences and the expectation that the group would all take responsibility for considering the effect of these on their work and relationships. It was acknowledged that the supervisor had major responsibility for this in her role with the group. The group had also identified gender beliefs from their communities and families of origin, and considered how these might affect their current behaviour, views of family life and relationships (see Burck and Daniel 1994).

When carrying out this exercise with people from differing cultural and ethnic backgrounds, assumptions about 'gender' across culture can be investigated. Surprises arise when similarities of experience are noted or discovery is made that the 'truth' about men and women is culturally situated. Similarly, an exploration of participants' 'cultural genograms' (Hardy and Laszloffy 1995), while undertaken with the aim of increasing trainees' awareness of their own cultural premises, can also explore a view of gender as a facet of culture. Trainees can be invited to form and ask questions that also address the interaction of class, role, sexuality and gender within their own families and communities.

These exercises begin to provide a *context* and *language* for continuing to explore these dimensions in connection with the group and families presenting for therapy.

Case example

Two children were referred to the clinic by their family doctor. The eldest, an 11-year-old boy, was seen as unhappy and aggressive at school, while his sister (8 years old) had a number of somatic complaints that have been investigated regularly by the general practitioner. The parents had been brought up in India, the children had been born in England.

From initial telephone contact it emerged that the couple wished to be seen separately in the first instance. They indicated that they were in considerable conflict, and that verbal communication between them was often passed through their son.

It emerged from talking with both mother and children that the father was being physically violent to his wife, and also to his son, and that this involved the use of kitchen implements and sticks. The father's view was that he had hit his wife, but a long time ago. His wife 'is stupid and cannot speak English properly', while he went to an English-speaking boarding school. He felt that she undermined and provoked him.

This relationship appeared to be replicated in his relationship to the (Japanese female) trainee therapist. After the first interview he phoned to speak to the white male psychiatrist (trainee) in the supervision group and complained that the female trainee could not speak English properly, was stupid and did not understand his position.

The family had all been subject to racism in this country. The father gave the impression of feeling powerless in his life outside the family.

Clearly, the dynamics with this family can be examined from gendered perspectives. The violence between the parents cannot be seen as unique, but rather as a relationship which '*in extremis* exemplifies the stereotypical gender arrangements that structure intimacy between men and women generally' (Goldner *et al.* 1990). The differential response of the son and daughter ('acting out' and 'internalising' behaviour) may also be seen as typically gendered responses. By belittling the female psychologist, bypassing the supervisor and asking to speak to the male team member, the father could be seen to conform to sexist views about gender and status. (On previous occasions, the team had been somewhat amused and curious when families assumed that the male member of the team was the supervisor, prior to introductions. On these occasions the role of the supervisor has been explained.)

Discussions within teams working with violence can become polarised, and this team was no exception. Initially, participants were trying to take 'neutral', 'systemic' stances towards the parents' relationship, considering the complementarity between the wife's behaviour and husband's response. The supervisor then invited them to consider the meaning and consequences of ignoring context and power difference between the couple. This led to a swing in viewing the relationship between wife and husband as victim and victimiser. The man in the group had powerful feelings about his own violence towards the husband, whereas one woman felt the wife should go to a woman's group in order to feel empowered enough to stand up to her husband and to get herself and her children to safety. Discussing the excellent papers from the Gender and Violence Project at the Ackerman Institute for the Family (Goldner 1998; Goldner *et al.* 1990) provided the opportunity for team members to consider a both/and approach to using feminist, systemic and social constructionist ideas and techniques in our work with this family. The project's work brings a welcome clarity to the field without minimising the complexities involved.

To view the interaction of family, team and supervisor only from the perspective of gender would be to become reductionist in another direction however. The influence of the culture and ethnicity of all participants was another lens through which the team could examine the dynamics and process of their work. The following section offers the reader the opportunity to consider their responses to the following dilemmas and issues. As discussed previously, 'difference' between peoples, whether of culture, ethnicity or gender, conveys different levels of power and status. The supervisor, psychologist and family all had different cultural backgrounds, but only the supervisor was from the dominant culture and ethnicity within the UK. Indeed, her own cultural background included a history of colonialism involving the family's home country of India. The supervisor was in the privileged position of having no experience of racism, while both the therapist and family had ample familiarity with it. Indeed, the husband's dismissal of his wife and therapist for not speaking 'proper English' could be seen as a type of internalised racism which would affect his view of himself in addition to others.

The dilemma for the supervisor was deciding how to use her own power beneficially to attend to the power imbalances in relation to the therapist and family. How could her experiences of sexism be helpful? How possible would it be to use her experience and knowledge to 'empower' the therapist and family, and how might the supervision group be usefully involved?

The supervisor was faced with the possible ethical implications for this service if the father refused to work with this practitioner on racial or gender grounds. Could the service refuse to offer an alternative therapist, particularly when the referred clients were children? Would we work with the mother and children alone, and what binds would that place us in? As importantly, the situation was a very difficult one for the psychologist, who was being attacked in a very public way at a time when she was feeling deskilled in her family therapy practice. It was important to raise the question of whether she wished to refuse to work with him or whether the supervisor and team could support her in unpacking sexism and racism as integral elements in this family's difficulties. If this could be achieved, her own knowledge of immigration, living in another culture and experience of racism and sexism might be very helpful to this family.

Ideas of 'empowering' women in violent relationships need some deconstruction also. Lau (1994) believes that the idea that women can only be empowered if they espouse the values and practices of Western feminists, derived from Western cultural traditions, is both insulting and racist. The mother in this family was not requesting the cessation of violence either for herself or for her son, but wanted to be able to talk with her husband rather than pass information through the son. If she were in India, she said she would go home to her family for a period of time in which the families could help negotiate around their difficulties. She hoped the team could negotiate on her behalf.

In this context the supervisor and team had to decide (and indeed had the power to decide) which was the highest 'context marker', 'culture' or women and children's safety in context of physical abuse. The concern about safety was such that they discussed involving social services to protect her son and herself, to which she agreed. With her request in mind, the services attempted to work together to help negotiate a different relationship within the family, including consulting mother's sister (in the US) and involving a refuge service for 'Asian' women to offer direct help to the mother. A male co-therapist was included in the work as it was felt that the father might then be more able to engage with the therapy. Careful consideration needed to be given to the way this was introduced and to the process of the co-working relationship (particularly in relation to gender, culture, ethnicity) so as not to undermine the therapist.

This case illustrates dilemmas for clients, therapists and supervisors in negotiating the complexities of working with 'difference'. Gendered analysis needs to include gender from many different viewpoints.

Power, hierarchy and supervision

In recently reviewing a tape on supervision, made in the early 1980s, with a group of current trainee supervisors, the changes that have taken place in the intervening years show themselves in a variety of ways. Current reactions to 'old-style techniques' included amazement at the degree to which the supervisors, as well as the therapists, saw themselves as 'experts' and used hierarchically orchestrated interventions from supervisor to therapist to family.

The current fashion in the UK for conversational, language-based therapies places less emphasis on instrumental, orchestrative, strategic or structural models. It is currently seen as desirable to increase therapist self-reflexivity and use of self (as opposed to use of technique) and decrease the hierarchy both between therapist and client, and within supervision teams.

The perspectives of power, hierarchy and involvement are, however, important dimensions in any supervisory relationship. Elsa Jones (1993) has clearly described how a pretence of democracy or equality will not work in the supervisor relationship. The trainee can be placed in a bind if she is meant to be more equal with the trainer, who frequently has greater experience and knowledge and certainly has more structural power. Ignoring these dimensions is more likely to lead to abuse of power than pretending equality. As McCann has described, however (see Chapter 4), the form that the hierarchy takes can change. In the initial stages of supervision, control will need to remain tightly in the supervisor's hands, with the relationship evolving into a consultancy role by the end of a qualifying training.

Nelson and Holloway (1990) have described three different types of power in supervisory relationships. The type most frequently considered is 'legitimacy'; it is earned by virtue of the supervisor's role *vis-à-vis* the trainee's. The supervisor has clinical responsibility for cases and can make decisions and overrule the trainees views. She has the responsibility and the power to assess, pass or fail students, and thus students may find it hard to challenge the supervisor too directly. Although this power has the possibility of misuse, it can also offer trainees, often in senior and responsible jobs in other contexts, the opportunity to relax into their trainee learning position.

'Referent' power is influence based on care and trust developed in a relationship; it is earned through trustworthy relating. Where the relationship of trainee and supervisor is 'good enough', this care and trust can allow the trainee to take risks and experiment outside of their usual range of skill. When 'legitimate' power predominates, and there is little trust or care, experimentation will be at a low premium.

'Expert' power is influence based on the knowledge and expertise of the supervisor; it is earned through education, training, experience and the communication of those to trainees.

The attention to hierarchy, power and influence in supervision may need to take different shape for men and women – women, traditionally not in powerful roles, may need to take more authority and power, while men may need to divest themselves of it (Burck and Daniel 1994). It might be expected that women supervisors may have been socialised to rely more on referent power as a means of influencing trainees, while men may have been socialised to using expert or legitimate power. This was not borne out, however, by a study by Robyak, Goodyear and Prange (1987), who found that males and inexperienced supervisors preferred to use the referent power styles with trainees.

Supervision is a reciprocal relationship like any other – the trainee will also be operating according to their own needs and expectations of the process. Trainees attributed more influence to supervisors of the same gender as themselves than to other gender supervisors and reported closer relationships with them (Worthington and Stern 1985), which might suggest a welcome 'fit' between the supervisor's style of using their power and influence and their own. This may also explain why trainees in same-sex supervisory relationships indicated more improvement in skills than did those in other-sex supervisory relationships (Worthington and Stern 1985).

Male supervisors may feel in a bind in regard to their use of power and authority. For example, a male supervisor directly intervened in a therapeutic session when a female trainee in the final stages for a therapy session started to devise an inappropriate task that had not been agreed beforehand. During the post-session discussion, the other trainees in the team expressed some disquiet since they, like the trainee herself, noticed a difference in the style and behaviours of the supervisor. The supervisor discussed the thinking behind his action, but the trainees, three female and one male, continued to challenge the supervisor's decision to intervene so directly, since it was felt to have undermined the trainee's therapeutic relationship with the clients. Is this an example of a male supervisor reinforcing the male/female hierarchy in addition to the supervisor/trainee hierarchy?

In consultation with other supervisors after the event, the supervisor reflected on the dominant belief that there is a difference between action and delivery. In other words, the tone was seen as all-important. The supervisor in question continued to think about this dilemma in terms of whether it is really possible to act from a position of power, whatever the tone, in a way that does not automatically reinforce male supremacy and an entitlement to the use and abuse of power. Such debates need to continue within the field, especially as they incorporate ethical issues and dilemmas. The major part of a supervisor's job is to provide a context for learning. The challenge of bringing gender into training is to find methods 'which are powerful enough to make a difference and yet not overly prescriptive' (Burck and Daniel 1995, p.120). The supervisor needs to make the ability to deconstruct and question our own beliefs and assumptions an explicit part of supervisory contact. Trainees will take what they want and transfer to our own style and beliefs.

Conclusion

Family therapy has clearly changed considerably since early feminist critiques. The field has moved beyond a focus on differences between men and women to a relativist position 'which eschews any such categories and focuses on a multiplicity of meanings and experiences' (Burck and Daniel 1995). Feminist theorists and therapists also prepared the ground for considerations of power and difference in other areas, the self of the therapist/supervisor, and more collaborative practice with clients. Clearly change to take pride in.

However, there is nothing intrinsic in current 'post-modern' practice to ensure that therapists consider gendered positions as crucial (albeit socially constructed). This relies on the field in general and the individual therapist in particular. There is a danger of complacency, of a 'we've done that' belief in the field that may mean that the advances in understanding power and difference could slip away. A power-blind approach is most easily maintained by those in dominant groups. As today's supervisors and therapists, we need to be alert to what we are missing — which aspects of our practice will be critiqued by the therapists and supervisors of tomorrow?

References

Broverman, I., Broverman D., Clarkson, F.G., Rosenkrantz, P. and Vogel, S.R. (1970) 'Sex role stereotypes and clinical judgements of mental health.' *Journal of Consulting Psychology 34*, 1–7.

Burck, C. and Daniel, G. (1995) *Gender and Family Therapy*. London: Karnac Books.

Caust, B., Libow, V. and Ruskin, P. (1981) 'Challenges and promises of training women as family systems therapists.' *Family Process 20*, 439–447.

Down, G. (1992) 'The effect of training on the gender beliefs of family therapy trainees.' Unpublished dissertation MSc, Family Therapy Institute of Family Therapy, London.

Gilligan, C. (1982) *In a Different Voice: Psychological Theory and Women's Development.* London: Harvard University Press.

Goldner, V. (1988) 'Generation and gender: Normative and corrective hierarchies.' *Family Process 27*, 17–31.

Goldner, V. (1991) 'Feminism and systemic practice: Two critical traditions in transition.' *Journal of Family Therapy 13*, 95–104.

Goldner, V. (1998) 'The treatment of violence and victimisation in intimate relationships.' *Family Process 37*, 3, 263–286.

Goldner, V., Penn, P., Sheinberg, M. and Walker, G. (1990) 'Love and violence: Gender paradoxes in volatile attachments.' *Family Process 29*, 4, 343–364.

Gorell Barnes, G. (1994) 'Family therapy.' In M. Rutter, L. Henlor and E. Taylor (eds) *Child and Adolescent Psychiatry: Modern Approaches, 3rd Edn.* Oxford: Blackwell.

Gorell Barnes, G. (1996) 'Gender issues.' In R. Davies, G. Upton and V. Varma (eds) *The Voice of the Child.* London: Routledge.

Gorell Barnes, G. (1998) *Family Therapy in Changing Times.* Basingstoke: MacMillan.

Gorell Barnes, G. and Henesy, S. (1994) 'Reclaiming a female mind from the experience of sexual abuse.' In C. Burck and B. Speed (eds) *Gender, Power and Relationships.* London: Routledge.

Haley, J. (1985) *Problem Solving Therapy.* Harper.

Harding, S. (ed) (1987) *Feminism and Methodology: Social Science Issues.* Milton Keynes: Open University Press.

Hardy, K. and Laszloffy, T. (1995) 'The cultural genogram: Key to training culturally competent family therapists.' *Journal of Marital and Family Therapy 12,* 3, 227–237.

Hare-Mustin, R. and Maracek, J. (eds) (1990) *Making a Difference: Psychology and the Construction of Gender.* New Haven and London: Yale University Press.

Haste, H. (1987) 'Growing into rules.' In V. Bruner and H. Haste (eds) *The Child's Construction of the World.* London: Methuen.

Jones, E. (1990) 'Feminism and family therapy: Can mixed marriages work?' In R.J. Perelberg and A. Miller (eds) *Gender and Power in Families.* London: Tavistock/Routledge.

Jones, E. (1991) *Working with Adult Survivors of Childhood Abuse.* London: Karnac Books.

Jones, E. (1993) *Family Systemic Therapy: Developments in the Milan Systemic Therapies.* Chichester: Wiley.

Jones, E. (1995) 'The construction of gender in family therapy.' In C. Burck and B. Speed (eds) *Gender, Power and Relationships.* London: Routledge.

Lau, A. (1994) 'Gender, power and relationships.' In C. Burck and B. Speed (eds) *Gender, Power and Relationships.* London and New York: Routledge.

Lloyd, B. (1987) 'Social representations of gender.' In J. Bruner and H. Haste (eds) *The Child's Construction of the World.* London: Routledge.

Maccoby, E. (1988) 'Gender as a social category.' *Developmental Psychology 24,* 755–765.

MacKinnon, L. and Miller, D. (1987) 'The new epistemology and the Milan approach: Feminism and sociopolitical considerations.' *Journal of Marital and Family Therapy 13,* 139–155.

Madanes, C. (1981) *Strategic Family Therapy.* San Francisco: Jossey Bass.

Minuchin, S. and Minuchin, P. (1974) *Families and Family Therapy.* Cambridge, Mass: Harvard University Press.

Nelson, M.L. and Holloway, E.L. (1990) 'Relation of gender to power and involvement in supervision.' *Journal of Counselling Psychology 37,* 473–481.

Parsons, T. and Bales, R.F. (1955) *Family, Socialisation, and Interactive Process.* Greencoe, Illinois: Free Press.

Robyak, J.E., Goodyear, R.K. and Prange, M.E. (1987) 'Effects of gender, supervisor and presenting problems: A practical students' reference for interpersonal power bases.' *Journal of Counselling Psychology 33*, 159–163.

Skynner, A.C.R. (1976) *One Flesh; Separate Persons: Principals of Family and Marital Psychotherapy.* London: Comfortable.

Speed, B. (1991) 'Reality exists OK? An argument against constructivism and social constructionism.' *Journal of Family Therapy 13*, 395–411.

Steadman, C. (1985) 'Listen how the caged bird sings: Amarjit's Song.' In C. Steadman, C. Urwin and V. Walkerdine (eds) *Language, Gender and Childhood.* London: Routledge and Kegan Paul.

Walters, M. (1990) 'A feminist perspective in family therapy.' In R.J. Perelberg and A.C. Miller (eds) *Gender and Power in Families.* London: Routledge.

Walters, M., Carter, B., Papp, P. and Silverstein, O. (1988) *The Invisible Web: Gender Patterns in Family Relationships.* New York: Guildford Press.

Weiner, P. and Boss, P. (1985) 'Exploring gender bias against women: Ethics for marriage and family therapy.' *Counselling and Values 30*, 1, 9–23.

Wheeler, D., Myers Avis, J., Miller, L. and Chaney, S. (1986) 'Rethinking family therapy education and supervision: A feminist model.' *Journal of Psychotherapy and the Family 1*, 53–71.

Winnicott, D.W. (1960) 'Ego distortion in sense of true and false self.' In *The Maturational Processes and the Facilitating Environment.* London: Hogarth Press.

Worthington, E.L. Jr. and Stern, A. (1985) 'The effects of supervisor and supervisee degree level and gender on the supervisory relationship.' *Journal of Counselling Psychology 32*, 3, 252–262.

8

Sex and Sexuality: The Supervisory Challenge

Damian McCann, Gill Gorell Barnes and Gwynneth Down

Introduction

Sex, sexuality, acts of intercourse and their many variations require attention to specificity of difference that family therapists as a whole have tended to ignore both at the theoretical and practice level. The shift from technique-based approaches to collaboration and the integration of self-in-system raises interesting questions for practitioners and supervisors alike. Are current supervisory endeavours helping practitioners to incorporate the sexual self-in-system(s) or are they consigning it to the margins of thinking and practice? Current debates within the field regarding the personal/professional and public/private divide seems central to any examination of sex and sexuality and will undoubtedly be influenced by conversations taking place at the societal level. How, then, do supervisors place sexuality as one of the many conversations about the self in therapy?

With these questions in mind, this chapter will examine ways in which sex and sexuality can become an active part of the supervisory process. The impact of more open conversations on the emerging supervisory relationship will be explored. Are there limits to such a discourse, and if so, what might these be? Issues and dilemmas relating to a number of case examples will be explored and suggestions advanced for incorporating sex and sexuality into the supervisory framework.

Defining sexuality

The Concise Oxford Thesaurus's (1996) definition of sexuality is based on differences in relation to sex, gender and sexual characteristics. Such a definition includes sexual desire, sexual appetite, sexiness, carnality, physicality, eroticism, lust, sensuality, sexual orientation and sexual preference.

Although dynamic in origin, sex and sexuality, historically, have been the subject of social control, especially when personal behaviour and public morality are not considered to be in step with one another. The well-known cliché 'No sex please, we're British', to some extent, captures this nation's position. The sensitivities surrounding any discussion of sex and sexuality in the public arena may also be responsible for systemic practitioners failing to raise the profile of sexuality generally within the therapeutic and supervisory relationship. However, developments relating to gender (where women have reclaimed their minds and bodies), the increasing diversity of family life and the greater visibility of lesbian and gay people within the therapeutic domain challenges practitioners to think beyond the neat constructions and conventions that relate specifically to hetero-sexual, monogamous, intact, nuclear family patterns of relating.

Accounting for the failure of systemic practitioners to work with sex and sexuality

Although, to some extent, the reticence of systemic therapists to raise sexual matters in their therapeutic and supervisory practice may be in line with other dominant voices within society that shy away from more straightforward liber-ating discourses, it is possible that aspects specific to the context in which systemic therapists practice also play a part in this avoidance behaviour. For instance, the context of family work suggests that sensitive matters relating to sex and sexuality should not, for parents, be discussed in front of the children, and for adolescents, be discussed in front of parents and siblings. Also, in situations where marital or sexual issues have emerged, family and systemic practitioners may have decided on strategic parental work, thereby downplaying the sexual aspects of the work. There also appears to be an assumption that attending to gender in the therapeutic encounter somehow incorporates sexuality and, for that matter, sex. In other words, they are treated as one and the same.

Furthermore, the over-sensitivity or absence of knowledge relating to cross-cultural practice amplifies practitioners' lack of confidence in tackling sex and sexuality within families where this may be a consideration. Krause (1998) suggests that we, as therapists, may not have the awareness of the general social and cultural processes which provide the context for the personal relationships of our clients.

To some extent, the over-reliance on model or technique within systemic practice has stood in the way of a more thorough consideration of sex and sexuality. For instance, in a recent video recording (*I'd Hear Laughter*, 1995) Insoo Kim Berg, who is seen working with two heterosexual parents and their 14-year-old daughter, asks the now infamous 'miracle question'. In response to the question 'Who will notice first that the miracle has happened for them?', the wife says that she will notice that her (unemployed) husband is up and ready to go. Insoo asks what differences the husband will notice about his wife that will let him know that the miracle has happened for her. He hesitates and then says that she will wake him with a kiss. 'So suppose she does wake you with a kiss, what will you do?' He says he will kiss her back. Insoo asks what will come next. He eventually says (in a barely audible voice) that they will fool around. Insoo, smiling, then remarks: 'So that is how you two will get up?' No further reference is made to the parents' marital/sexual relationship since the focus shifts to the daughter's non-attendance at school. In other words, the reliance on solution talk in respect of the presenting problem guides the therapist's decision not to enter the more thorny issue relating to sex.

This example does however raise some interesting questions about the extent to which sexuality, as a topic, should be a contained conversation with a couple and when it might become the domain of family conversation. At the same time, it is possible that the therapeutic setting itself, particularly in regard to one-way screens and video technology, does not constitute a safe or intimate environment for the exploration of these matters.

The supervisory context

Burck and Daniel (1995) have commented on the way that clinical supervision groups can offer an intimate context in which the sharing of beliefs and assumptions about race, gender and sexuality can be explored. However, the extent to which this is fostered depends largely on the supervisor's own relationship to, and comfort with, the subject. Supervisors may, for instance, adopt any of the following positions. They may adopt a 'proactive' stance, whereby they take responsibility in introducing sex and sexuality at an early stage in the proceedings. On the other hand, supervisors may take a more 'reactive' stance, choosing only to deal with sex and sexuality when this arises in the clinical work or when trainees make reference to it in their discussions within the group. Finally, supervisors may decide on a 'retrospective' stance, dealing with issues after the event or when it becomes apparent that something important has been missed.

Essentially, it is the job of supervisors to find a bridge between the private, secret, sexual self of the trainees and the more public domain where sexuality can become an active ingredient in the therapeutic and supervisory relationships.

Supervisors themselves need to be aware that even when they fail to raise the profile of sex within the supervision group, sexuality will still be present, for example in coded language or double entendres. Part of the difficulty, which both supervisors and their students share, is the absence of a formal language in which to access thoughts and feelings about sex and sexuality, but another difficulty relates to the act of self-disclosure. In other words, developing a language and confidence in opening conversations about sex and sexuality although, on a content level, enriching to the life of a supervision group, on a process level, risks the raising of eyebrows since, at the same time, it communicates personal information about the informant. By constructing more informed conversations about sexuality as a part of what is in the therapeutic mind, it becomes less likely that therapists or supervisors unwittingly find themselves caught in layers of 'repressed discourses' from earlier in their lives. Prurient, 'flip' remarks, disconnections and 'giggling' are less likely to occur. It also enables therapists to challenge clients who are themselves inappropriately involved in giving details of their sexual encounters. As one supervisor helpfully commented to a colleague: 'Who is it that is getting off on this conversation?'

The challenge therefore concerns the opening of such conversations in a way that draws trainees out and extends their thinking and practice. At the same time it also requires a level of supervisor knowledge and alertness so that assumptions are challenged. For instance, during one supervision group the supervisor was struck by the ease with which the trainees developed hypotheses about a mother and her 10-year-old son who was getting into trouble at school. These hypotheses centred entirely on the supposed absent father. Nothing in the language of the group suggested an awareness that the mother might be lesbian or that her son might be the product of donor insemination. If trainees are not entertaining such thoughts, then it is possible that the institutions in which they train are not entertaining such thoughts, and if this is so, then, assuming the mother is a lesbian and the son a product of donor insemination, how will they be enabled to share this information? One of the dangers of silence is that it further reinforces earlier messages that a 'hidden' aspect of a relationship cannot be spoken about.

Learning the language

Case study number one

Jane, aged 9 years old, is referred to a Child and Family Consultation Service. She is refusing to attend school and has also become clingy towards her mother. Jane's mother and father separated three years ago. She has regular contact with her father. Jane and her mother, Elizabeth, are invited to the session. The trainee, one of three students in training to become a family and systemic therapist, is being supervised from behind the one-way screen by a supervisor who is using an earbug. On collecting the family from the waiting room, the student discovers that the mother has brought a female friend called Donna. Elizabeth insists that Donna join them for the session. Once in the room, the trainee ignores Donna and addresses all her comments to Elizabeth and Jane. One of the trainees observing the session from behind the one-way screen comments on Donna's 'butchness'.

Although the supervisor sent a message through the earbug to the trainee asking her to enquire about Donna's presence in the session and the meaning of this, the trainee continued to struggle in directly addressing Donna. The trainee was asked to take an inter-session break. During the break the trainee was asked to explain why it was that Donna was present and why the trainee was having such difficulty establishing Donna's relationship to Elizabeth and Jane. The trainee explained that she felt uncomfortable asking such questions as she did not want to be seen to be making assumptions. On closer examination, it became apparent that the trainee was struggling to find a way of asking the question of Donna's affiliation that would not presuppose that she and Elizabeth were in a lesbian relationship.

This particular case scenario raises a number of interesting dilemmas. For instance, it highlights a level of discomfort in the trainee that may be more about her own homophobia than about finding an appropriate language to enquire. For even when the trainee returned to the session armed with suggestions for addressing Donna's relationship with Elizabeth and Jane, she still struggled to ask. Eventually it became apparent that Donna was in fact the mother's best friend and Elizabeth had asked her to come because she was feeling nervous about the appointment. As far as could be ascertained, Donna and Elizabeth were not lovers. Nevertheless, the question remains as to whether the trainee would have struggled as much were Donna a man.

Exercise number one

Consider how, as a supervisor, you would handle the trainee therapist's decision not to include Donna in the session. How might you address the comment relating to Donna being 'butch', made by the trainee behind the one-way screen?

Exercise number two

Role play the scenario outlined in the case study above. Provide the trainees with a basic outline of the case. Do not tell them that Donna is about to arrive with Elizabeth and Jane.

For maximum effectiveness it is best to ask for two trainees to play the family and at the same time a further trainee can be identified to assist in getting Elizabeth and Jane into role. That trainee will obviously become Donna. (The family and Donna are encouraged not to make their relationship clear unless asked questions that specifically address their affiliation. For instance, if asked how they would describe their relationship, they might answer that they are good friends. The therapist must be forced to work to find a specific question that will help him/her clarify their actual relationship.) Get two of the remaining students to work together. One will become the therapist and the other will act as a consultant to the therapist.

Usually the trainee who becomes the therapist will be thrown off balance when confronted with the arrival of Donna.

The whole point of this exercise is for the trainee therapist, and to some extent the consultant, to struggle in finding a confidence in asking difficult, and at times uncomfortable, questions.

Following the role play, there can be an open discussion within the group.

To some extent, supervisors will be assisted in their task by sound training and teaching on other aspects of the course. For instance, Crowe and Ridley (1990), when training couple and sex therapists, suggest that there should be formal teaching in the following areas:

- knowledge of sexual anatomy and physiology
- varieties of sexual experiences including cultural influences and sexual variations

- myths of sexuality
- the Master's and Johnson approach
- physical treatments for sexual inadequacy
- relationship problems and their relevance to sexuality.

Although this may be considered by some systemic supervisors as irrelevant to their particular context, the advantage of such training is that it creates a secure knowledge base in regard to sex and sexuality from which trainees can draw in their work with individuals, couples and families. Crowe and Ridley advocate this teaching on the basis that trainees in general couple therapy need to develop a sense of confidence in dealing with sexual matters so as to help couples who themselves may be somewhat self-conscious about discussing intimate sexual details. Where therapists are more open and comfortable with their own sexuality this enables clients in turn to feel more at ease.

Exercise number three

In order to place sex and sexuality firmly on the agenda within any supervisory group, supervisors will need to decide to set aside a block of time in which to address the trainees' issues and questions. One way of doing this can be to declare that language for sexual behaviours should be part of a therapist's repertoire. To develop this language trainees may be asked to work in pairs and to identify as many 'pseudonyms' that they can think of that specifically refer to sexual parts or sexual acts. Once these have been named, the supervisor can get the trainees back in pairs to role play a situation where one trainee uses a pseudonym such as naughty cuddles, having your oats, a bit of nookie, a Sunday special or dipping the wick, and the therapist attempts to clarify exactly what it is they are saying. For example, in a recent interview with a heterosexual couple, the man in the relationship mentioned the fact that he and his female partner rarely get physical. As they had been talking about conflict, the therapist assumed that he was speaking about violence. It was only later in the interview when the therapist ventured to ask about their sexual relationship that the male client pointed out that he had already told the therapist about this. The point of this exercise is to give trainees the opportunity of learning to talk directly about sex and to alert them to the existence of sex and sexuality within the domain of the couple relationship and of the therapeutic and supervisory relationship.

Previous attempts to put sex and sexuality on the agenda have included trainees watching many hours of desensitising sex videos. However, the extent to which this assists in the development of a meaningful dialogue is open to question. One of the authors recalls watching, on video, many different acts of sex without really discovering anything about her own sexuality. Although 'group discussions' accompanied these, the context biased towards senior male practitioners was constraining rather than freeing. In using visual aids for training, careful thought needs to be given to the gendered composition of the discussion groups as well as to the generational mix and related professional power. The reluctance of systemic practitioners to enter the domain of sexual choices and preferences as part of therapy, and being willing to consider the effects as well as the absences of sexual behaviours, may be less about informed choice and more about anxiety, ignorance and cultural as well as internal prohibitions.

Issues of self-disclosure

McCann (1998) suggests that there appears to be two quite distinct schools of thought concerning the therapist's disclosure of personal information during the course of therapy, although these can be conceptualised as opposite ends of a continuum. At one end lie those views which positively discourage therapists sharing any personal information with clients on the basis that it interferes with the therapeutic encounter. For instance, it is believed that therapist's self-disclosure cuts across the client's own agenda and may stimulate the client's wish to know more, a point further underlined by Plummer (1995), who suggests that 'secrecy may create necessary social boundaries' and that the act of 'telling all' renders people extremely vulnerable. At the opposite end of the continuum are those (Hildebrand 1998) who encourage the sharing of selected aspects of self on the basis that it serves to enhance the process of engagement and makes the whole training and therapeutic endeavour more authentic.

The relevance of this debate for supervisory relationships is that trainees and supervisors face the same dilemmas as therapists and clients in regard to where to position themselves on the secrecy and self-disclosure continuum. At the same time, the move towards greater openness within training, designed to bridge the gap between the personal and the professional and create more integrated and effective practitioners, is not without its problems. A position of transparency, although consistent with post-modern thinking where the emphasis is towards co-construction and collaboration involving not only mind and method but also the therapist as a human interacting system (McCann 1998), may need careful consideration. Disclosure operates on a number of levels and may create tensions and difficulties within supervisory groups, particularly if some trainees are more open than others. Similarly, the transparency of a supervisor, although helpful in one sense, may also compromise his/her position and authority within the group, particularly if there are issues about a supervisor's own sexuality which feel unresolved. However, it is also worth remembering Watzlawick, Beavers and Jackson's (1967) now infamous injunction that 'no matter how one may try, one cannot not communicate' (p.49), a point that has been further elaborated by Taylor *et al.* (1998), who suggest that 'we constantly give things away, our gender, skin colour, class, our attitudes and beliefs, and, for those who speak the language, no doubt our sexuality' (p.10).

Questions therefore are less concerned with whether sex and sexuality are dynamic components in a supervisory context since we would each assume that they are. However, they emerge more around how such private components of self should be made explicit and assessed in the context of their relevance to therapeutic work in regard to intimate human relationships. Supervisors also have a responsibility to make supervisees aware of the potential consequences for public openness (Long 1997). Given the sensitivities and dilemmas involved in self-disclosure of any kind, but particularly around sex, sexuality and secrets, both for the self and in the family of the trainee, it is suggested that careful attention must be paid to creating a safe context for any meaningful and relevant exploration.

Exercise number four

An explanation of the emerging sexual self in different family and peer group systems can begin to create such a context.

In pairs or small groups, consider the following questions:

When did you first become conscious of yourself as a sexual being?

What were the messages you received about this emerging sexual self?

What conversations did you have with others about your sexuality?

What challenges have you negotiated to get to where you are now in regard to your sexuality and the expression of this?

How comfortable are you doing this exercise?

Trainees may decide to use a genogram, mind map or some other symbolic means for plotting the development of their sexuality.

This should then link with the next exercise.

A variation on the above exercise concerns trainees' and supervisors' comfort or discomfort in talking about a range of sexual practices. Although sex is now discussed, detailed and shown within the media (newspapers, literature and television), sexual practices are still generally seen as private, and little is known about what is done, where, when and by whom. Therefore, clients, therapists, trainees and supervisors may hold a variety of beliefs about which aspects of sexual life and practice should be considered personal.

Exercise number five

As part of opening the subject of sexual practice, trainees may be asked, in pairs, to address the following questions:

> *With whom have you discussed your own sexual practices?*
>
> *What did you notice about this? For example, are you more or less likely to discuss sex with your sexual partner than with your close friends?*
>
> *How detailed have these discussions been?*
>
> *What do these conversations tell you about your beliefs relating to the different contexts in which sex can or cannot be discussed?*

This exercise may help therapists to consider how particular contexts and relationships give meaning to discussions about sexual practices. Trainees can be asked to consider the context of therapy and how, as trainee therapists, they develop therapeutic relationships with clients that actually facilitate discussions of sex when appropriate.

Exercises such as these should prevent trainees feeling uncomfortable when discussing sexual practices with clients, whatever their sexual orientation, or being frightened of showing ignorance when it comes to working with clients who engage in sexual practices that fall outside the trainee's repertoire or awareness.

Exercise number six

A further consideration concerns the theory of sexual development that underpins trainees' work with individuals, couples and families.

For example, how does the group respond to a referral of a trans-gendered person seeking therapy with her wife and sons?

Seek each person's views separately before generating group discussion.

Long (1997) suggests that supervisors who address issues related to sexual orientation encourage supervisees to learn about difference, accept difference and develop an awareness of their personal biases regarding sexual orientation. She also advocates self-examination as a necessary step in preparing supervisors to work with supervisees who may hold different values and opinions than themselves (Long 1996).

Case study number two

Brian, a gay man in his forties, was fighting to retain his right to have a committed relationship with his partner Dwayne and to be free to cruise from time to time. He wanted to flirt and engage in sex with other men: 'I do not want to feel my definition of myself as a sexual being is tied into one relationship.' The therapist, a heterosexual female, thought that this may be linked to a fear of losing Dwayne, since Brian had previously had a long relationship with someone who concealed his HIV status until three weeks before he died. However, the therapist was fearful of imposing her particular framework on the problem, particularly as this was not the issue Dwayne was raising in their couples therapy. Dwayne was very upset with Brian's new position and felt it was a rejection of their relationship. He questioned why Brian needed to go outside their relationship for sex. Was it because he, Dwayne, was not attractive enough?

In a conversation between Siegel and Walker (1996), Siegel, in thinking about the meanings of sex to gay men and the way in which sexual experimentation operates, suggests, in relation to 'cruising', that 'each sexual encounter offers the opportunity to claim what has been buried, hidden, denied, or repressed' (p.35). In addition, he suggests that 'the process of claiming one's forbidden homosexuality involves getting to know many parts of the undiscovered self, through these temporary attractions to others' (p.35). The therapist, however, tended towards the hetero-normative position that 'cruising' unsettles and will not lead to happiness within the couple relationship. On this particular point Shernoff (1999) says: 'There is nothing that confuses heterosexual therapists more than working with male couples who are exploring the option of non-monogamy' (p.63). The reasons for this, according to Shernoff, are that it seems to challenge the most fundamental clinical assumptions that 'affairs' are symptoms of relationship trouble, where it is assumed that gay men are avoiding intimacy by triangulation. Morin (1999) reminds us of the following: 'Non-monogamous options are thoroughly woven into the tapestry of queer love and are lived out on a richly diverse continuum' (p.7).

The therapist, who was part of a supervision group, sought supervision in relation to her own feelings about Brian's wish to open the relationship and Dwayne's difficulty with this. Members of the group reflected on the therapist's dilemma. They were interested in gender discourses and the ways in which they link with sexuality, i.e. a gendered, masculine discourse about freedom. If the therapist were male, would she have been more joined to Brian's position than to Dwayne's 'female ethic' of commitment and security? This point was challenged on the grounds that it did not reflect the position of men in relationships statistically, in that, it is men who appear to seek marriage and remarriage and who perhaps long for security. Women are now finding more public voices about sex and love not having to be connected in ways that were formally seen as more characteristic of men. The problem arises, perhaps, when there are two men vying to be in charge of the definition of the relationship. It was noted that heterosexuals often define gay male relationships in a rather gendered, stereotyped way, namely that there has to be a 'man' and a 'woman'. The therapist suggested that a central issue for her concerned the connection between the development of intimacy and the inter-penetration of bodies. Group members reflected on conservative, conventional voices fighting with more radical, 'liberating' beliefs about the conduct of relationships. It was noted that even within the gay community there are many positions and 'marginalised voices'. Dwayne's position could be seen as too restrictive and possibly even homophobic among those in post-modern gay life who argue against exclusive attachments and look instead to different expressions of self-realisation.

The group also wondered whether the presenting issue 'of fidelity' was really the issue. Was the sexual issue the hook on which other aspects of the relationship and other unresolved issues were being hung? One group member, who is gay, suggested working with the couple in terms of developing a fuller understanding of the beliefs underpinning their relationship, including an exploration of their expectations. The thinking behind this would be to challenge the couple to see their relationship as a dynamic living entity that will evolve and change over time. Rather than drifting into difficulties, perhaps the presenting dilemma offers them an opportunity to renegotiate a new way forward. This would concur with the belief that the times when opening up the relationship seems constructive, creative and functional are when the couple has an honest and positive level of communication (Shernoff 1999).

A third area for consideration concerned the therapist's own relationship to the material. Morin (1999) suggests 'Too often therapists fall into the trap of soothing their own discomfort with ambiguity by coaxing clients toward security, when helping them to tolerate increasing levels of uneasiness would promote more growth' (p.70). What, then, in the therapist's own material might be relevant to her struggle with Brian and Dwayne? The therapist was asked whether there might be anything in her own background experience that influenced or organised her thinking about this couple and their relational dilemma. The therapist spoke of her father and the stories that she had learned as a child which alluded to, but never spoke openly of, his friendships with men. Also, the meanings attached to his many night-time absences from home were quite confusing. For instance, her mother would refer to his wish to have Turkish baths, which seemed to go on all night, contributing both to a mythic significance and possible infidelity to her. However, it was only when her parents divorced, her father suffered from depression and subsequently fell in love with his male psychiatrist, that the therapist really became aware of her father's sexuality. Nevertheless, this was not openly spoken about in the home, and it was only years later that her mother confided the actual details of the story. For instance, she spoke of the dangers entailed when the therapist's father went 'cottaging'. Apparently, he was arrested on two occasions, taken to court and only escaped a prison sentence by enlisting the help of other influential friends who lied on his behalf. The therapist also, for the first time, learned of the occasions her father had been beaten up for soliciting.

Not surprisingly, the therapist's own background history contributed significantly to her feelings and response to Brian's wish to open his relationship and the impact this might have on Dwayne. Brian could be seen to be associated with the therapist's father in her own story, and, given the tangible suffering and dangers involved for her father and the eventual impact of this on her parents' relationship, it is hardly surprising that she believed that cruising unsettles and will ultimately have a detrimental effect on the relationship between Brian and Dwayne. How, then, would such a therapist help a couple who, for any number of reasons, may need to face the challenge of opening their relationship? Morin (1999), for instance, reminds us that most gay men who open the door to outside sex are, among other things, 'searching for solutions to common, intransigent problems, such as erotic incompatibilities, significant desire discrepancies and, yes, the waning passions of long-term love' (p.71).

Therapists and supervisors, of whatever sexual orientation, have an ethical responsibility to face within themselves blocks that may be interfering in their work with others. For the therapist working with Brian and Dwayne, the supervisory relationship provided a safe environment in which she could explore aspects of her own story that impacted on her ability to work effectively with the couple seeking her help. Helping the therapist contextualise her father's unfortunate experiences prior to the legislation in the 1960s that decriminalised intimate sexual acts between men in private assisted her in revisiting the idea of sexual experiences in the public domain in the late 1990s. She was also

---

Exercise number seven

Supervisors will encourage their trainees to role play ways in which they would open this conversation with Brian and Dwayne.

Time should be allowed to process the issues that emerge, particularly in relation to the language the trainees use during their conversation with Brian and Dwayne.

---

encouraged to share her own position in relation to the issues Brian and Dwayne were presenting as a means of furthering the conversation and helping them decide whether they would like to continue working with her.

Conclusion

In this chapter, the authors suggest that sex and sexuality are dynamic components in any supervisory relationship. However, sensitivities, uneasiness and fear conspire to keep these supposed private and personal conversations out of the domain of systemic thinking and practice. Nevertheless, it is suggested that supervisors must endeavour to find a bridge between the private, secret, sexual self of the trainee and the more public arena where sexuality can become an active ingredient in the therapeutic and supervisory relationship. Self-examination is clearly important to any discussion, and a number of exercises are offered to assist in the process of actively engaging with trainees in this important, but much neglected, area of thinking and practice. At the same time, supervisors are reminded of their ethical and professional responsibilities in regard to self-disclosure and need to make supervisees aware of the potential consequences for public openness. Tensions inherent in the relationship between silence and openness will no doubt continue to challenge supervisors and their trainees for some time to come.

References

Berg, I.K. (1995) *I'd Hear Laughter! Finding Solutions for the Family.* A Brief Therapy Centre video tape. New York: W.W. Norton and Company inc.

Burck, C. and Daniel, G. (1995) *Gender and Family Therapy.* London: Karnac Books.

Concise Oxford Thesaurus. (1996) Oxford: Oxford University Press.

Crowe, M. and Ridley, J. (1990) *Therapy with Couples: A Behavioural Systems Approach to Marital and Sexual Problems.* Oxford: Blackwell.

Hildebrand, J. (1998) *Bridging the Gap: A Training Module in Personal and Professional Development.* London: Karnac Books.

Krause, I.B. (1998) *Therapy across Culture*. London: Sage Publications.

Long, J. (1996) 'Working with lesbians, gays, and bisexuals: Addressing hetero-sexism in supervision.' *Family Process 35*, 377–388.

Long, J. (1997) 'Sexual orientation: Implications for the supervisory process.' In T.C. Todd and C.L. Storm (eds) *The Complete Systemic Supervisor*. MA: Allyn and Bacon.

McCann, D. (1998) 'To say or not to say? Dilemmas in disclosing sexual orientation.' *Context 40*, December, 6–9.

Morin, J. (1999) 'Case commentary.' *Networker*. March/April. 70–71.

Plummer, K. (1995) *Telling Sexual Stories: Power, Change and Social Worlds*. London: Routledge.

Shernoff, M. (1999) 'Monogamy and gay men: When are open relationships a therapeutic option?' *Networker*, March/April, 63–70.

Siegel, S. and Walker, G. (1996) 'Connections: Conversations between a gay therapist and a straight therapist.' In J. Laird and R.J. Green (eds) *Lesbians and Gays in Couples and Families*. CA. Jossey Bass.

Taylor, G., Solts, B., Roberts, B. and Maddicks, R. (1998) 'A queer business: Gay clinicians working with gay clients.' *Clinical Psychology Forum 119*, 9–11.

Watzlawick, P., Beavers, J.B. and Jackson, D.D. (1967) *Pragmatics of Human Communication: A Study of Interactional Patterns, Pathologies and Paradoxes*. New York: Norton.

The Association for Family Therapy and Systemic Practice. The Red Book: Registration of Supervisors and Accreditation of Training Courses: Criteria and Guidelines

Section A: Registration of supervisors

1. Introduction

1.1. Following the establishment of clear criteria from AFT in relation to becoming a registered systemic/family therapist the CRED Committee commissioned a subcommittee to create criteria for the registration of supervisors. Registered supervisors would be eligible to supervise those who were training to become or were qualified as systemic/family therapists.

1.2. Training to become a supervisor must be both rigorous and flexible. A number of training institutes are already running courses for supervisors and it is important to develop a coherent set of criteria so that those entering such training can know how these courses will equip them to reach the desired level.

1.3 Since these criteria are being developed in a field which already contains many experienced practitioners it is intended that registration as a registered supervisor will be consistent with the present structure and procedures for registering as a systemic/family therapist.

1.4 It is intended that people wishing to register as a registered supervisor would complete their training with a training institution in a variety of ways unless they were eligible for grandparenting. The sections which follow are intended for individuals and for courses.

2. Definitions and criteria

A registered supervisor is a qualified system/family therapist who is eligible to:

2.1 supervise the clinical work of those people training for qualified family therapy status on an accredited course. i.e. post-foundation level;

2.2 provide supervision to qualified family therapists as part of their continuing professional development (as described in UKCP registration criteria).

3. Routes to registration

To be considered for registered supervisor status, individuals should:

3.1 satisfy the criteria for the grandparenting clause (see below)

   or

3.2 satisfactorily complete an accredited training (see below).

3.1 REGISTRATION THROUGH GRANDPARENTING

Applicants for registration through Grandparenting must:

   3.1.1 be registered as a systemic/family therapist;

3.1.2 describe the past and present history of their practice as a supervisor by demonstrating with evidence that they have been practising as a systemic/family therapy supervisor for a minimum of: *either*

    3.1.2.1. eight years when the experience of supervising is gained mainly outside formal training courses. This supervisory experience must have been in relation to the clinical work of systemic/family therapists who are now, in the main, registered but at the time relating to this application

        3.1.2.2.1. were approaching qualifying level

        3.1.2.3.2. had achieved qualifying level

        3.1.2.3.3. were eligible to be registered (if registration had existed prior to May 1993)

        3.1.2.1.4. were in the process of being registered

        3.1.2.1.5. are in the progress of registering now

or

    3.1.2.2. four years when the experience of supervision is gained mainly on courses training systemic/family therapists to qualifying level

or both;

3.1.3. demonstrate with evidence their involvement in on-going supervision of systemic/family therapy practice of at least eight hours per month post-foundation level;

3.1.4. demonstrate that they have had continuing and relevant professional development and education including continued knowledge of, and integration of, contemporary theory into practice;

3.1.5. show evidence of continuing competence in direct and indirect supervision (see definition below)

3.1.6. provide supporting evidence in the form of:

    3.1.6.1. the names of three referees who have direct knowledge of the applicant's past and current practice. One referee should be, or have been recently, in a position of consulting to the supervision of the applicant. One referee should be a peer who has qualified or might qualify for registration in his/her own right. One referee should be a past supervisee

    3.1.6.2. a curriculum vitae demonstrating those aspects of the applicant's work which are particularly relevant to this application, including training, publications, research and evidence of contribution to the development of systemic/family therapy supervision

    3.1.6.3. the registration panel reserves the right to seek further validation of the applicant's supervisory practice in a variety of ways.

3.2.REGISTRATION THROUGH A TRAINING COURSE

Accredited training course applicants must have satisfactorily completed an accredited training course in supervision. To train for registered supervisory status an applicant should be registered as a systemic/family therapist with UKCP and, usually, have completed a period of consolidation, including some experience of supervision. In the period of consolidation applicants should have continued to practise systemic/family therapy, preferably with a mixed client group.

4. Criteria for completion of training

At the end of their training an applicant for registered status must be able to demonstrate reflexive competence in the areas of practice, theory, personal development and ethics.

4.1   In the area of *practice* he/she must have the abilities to:

4.1.1. use a range of supervisory techniques in the supervision of systemic/family therapists

4.1.2. show a fit between the model of supervision and the model of therapy being used by the systemic/family therapy trainee

4.1.3. maintain appropriate boundaries within the supervision process

4.1.4. accepts appropriate clinical responsibility

4.1.5. create a positive environment for learning including taking appropriate risks

4.1.6. be supportively challenging of the trainee

4.1.7. sensitively handle the supervisor/supervisee relationship

4.1.8. enable trainees to monitor and review all aspects of the therapeutic process

4.1.9. effectively supervise trainees directly and indirectly (directly is taken to mean 'live', video or audio tape; indirectly is taken to mean discussion of a case)

4.1.10. understand group and individual processes and use them to promote the development of trainees over time.

4.2   In the area of *theory* he/she must have the abilities to:

4.2.1. articulate a clear understanding of the theory of supervision including relevant research

4.2.2. facilitate trainees to discriminate and use relevant theoretical constructs in their practice

4.2.3. promote the abilities of trainees to make useful connections between theory and practice

4.2.4. apply systemic theory to the process of training.

4.3.   In the area of *personal development* he/she must have the abilities to:

4.3.1. recognize and understand patterns from within their own significant relationship systems (past, present and future), and culture which may help and/or hinder their work with trainees

4.3.2. to demonstrate the effects of self-reflection and the recognition and understanding outlined in 4.3.1

4.3.3. facilitate trainees to recognize and understand patterns from within their own significant relationship systems (past, present and future), and culture which may help and/or hinder their work

4.3.4. to demonstrate these same abilities.

4.4. In the area of *ethics* he/she must be able to show:

4.4.1. adherence to a code of ethics approved by the Family, Couple, Sexual and Systemic (FCSS) section of UKCP

4.4.2. ability to promote anti-discriminatory practice

4.4.3. capacity to promote trainees abilities to reflect on their own therapeutic practice.

5. Components of training

5.1 Supervisory time (see table)

Supervisory time 320 hours		
DIRECT		**INDIRECT**
Minimum of 160 hours		Maximum of 160 hours
Minimum of 40 hours presented to the registered supervisor		Includes all other relevant and appropriate supervisory experiences: such as case discussion, simulations, observations
Minimum of 20 hours live	Maximum of 20 hours video/audio tape	

The training should include a minimum of 320 hours of supervision at post-foundation level, encompassing a range of supervisory experiences. The accumulation of hours refers not only to the number, but also to the coherence of those supervisory experiences:

5.1.1. of these 320 hours, a minimum of 160 hours should be direct ('live', video/audio) supervision, where the trainee supervisor is the primary person responsible for the supervision;

5.1.2. of these 160 hours, a minimum of 40 hours should be presented to the registered supervisor training them. Of these 40 hours:

5.1.2.1. a minimum of 20 hours should be 'live' work by the trainee supervisor in the presence of the registered supervisor training them.

5.1.2.2.   up to20 hours should be retrospective presentation to the registered supervisor of video/audio tape;

5.1.3.   the remaining 160 hours is indirect supervisory time (e.g. case discussion, use of simulations, observation of registered supervisor at work).

5.2.   The majority of supervisory hours (4.5.1 to 4.5.3) should be supervision of people considered to be in the final, advanced part of their systemic/family therapy training or equivalent.

5.3.   *Academic study:* should be a minimum of 150 hours in the ratio one-third contact time and two-thirds personal study.

5.4.   *Duration of training:* should usually be completed in not less than two and not more than three years.

5.5.   *Assessment:* The competencies of the supervisor in training should be assessed through methods designed by the course and which fit the above criteria.

APPENDIX II

Current Structure for Accreditation, Registration and Training of Family Therapists

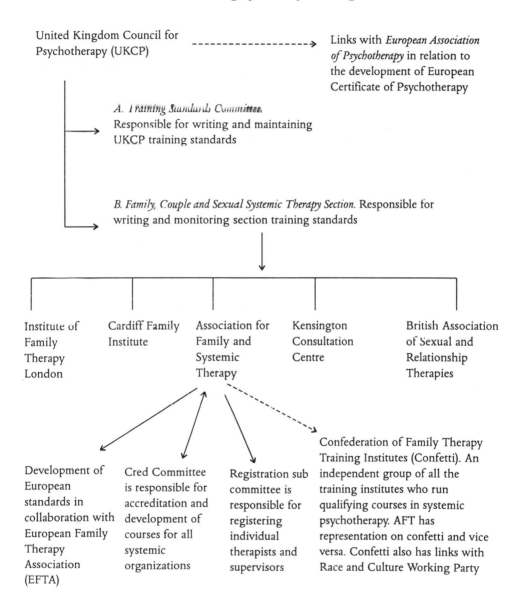

United Kingdom Council for Psychotherapy (UKCP)

Links with *European Association of Psychotherapy* in relation to the development of European Certificate of Psychotherapy

A. *Training Standards Committee*. Responsible for writing and maintaining UKCP training standards

B. *Family, Couple and Sexual Systemic Therapy Section.* Responsible for writing and monitoring section training standards

Institute of Family Therapy London

Cardiff Family Institute

Association for Family and Systemic Therapy

Kensington Consultation Centre

British Association of Sexual and Relationship Therapies

Development of European standards in collaboration with European Family Therapy Association (EFTA)

Cred Committee is responsible for accreditation and development of courses for all systemic organizations

Registration sub committee is responsible for registering individual therapists and supervisors

Confederation of Family Therapy Training Institutes (Confetti). An independent group of all the training institutes who run qualifying courses in systemic psychotherapy. AFT has representation on confetti and vice versa. Confetti also has links with Race and Culture Working Party

Source: Association for Family and Systemic Practice. *The Red Book: Registration of Supervisors and Accreditation of Training Courses Criteria and Guidelines* (1996)

Standard Letter

Dear ....

We have heard from .... that you have some concerns about
.... and that you would welcome some help from our team. We should
like to offer you an appointment on .... to discuss your concerns in
some detail.

For this first appointment we would particularly like to meet everyone who
lives in the household. We expect the meeting to last about 1¼ hours.

A member of our team will be meeting with you, and the other members of
the team will observe our discussion through a one-way screen. We find that
this is a good way for us to work as we are able to listen to, and think carefully
about, what you tell us and about how we may be able to help. With your
agreement, we like to make a videotape of the meeting so that we may review
it afterwards. Please telephone me before the appointment if there is anything
about our way of working that you would like to discuss.

I enclose a form which we would like you to complete and return as soon as
possible in the stamped addressed envelope.

The department is situated in the north part of the hospital. Please go to the
Main Entrance of the hospital and follow the signs or enquire at the Porters'
Lodge. I have enclosed a map to help you find your way.

We look forward to seeing you on the ....

Yours sincerely,

Enc: Questionnaire, SAE and Map

Points to Consider when Establishing Clinical Placements for Trainee Family Therapists

Introduction

The formalisation of training in family therapy has resulted in trainees approaching qualified family therapists in agency settings for the purpose of securing clinical placements. Forward-thinking agencies are valuing these opportunities as a rich source of ideas and a healthy challenge – something which may be good for an agency to offer.

A distinction needs to be drawn between trainees undertaking an introductory- or intermediate-level training and who are seeking a clinical placement, and those completing as advanced-level training. In addition, some advanced-level courses offer in-house supervision whilst others rely on externally-supervised placements. In view of this, it is important that prospective supervisors clarify the level of training supervision needed by a trainee before offering a clinical placement.

It is, of course, possible that some trainees may be seeking a clinical placement not for the purpose of qualifying within the field but seeking extra hours for their own personal and professional development. Other trainees will have their own home base to rely on throughout the course for the provision of ongoing clinical work. Those who have not, however, may well seek a clinical placement to fulfil the course requirements or to supplement the in-house supervision group.

It is also worth bearing in mind that students, in line with developments within the UKCP, will be seeking placements not only from the public sector, but also from the voluntary and private sectors.

In considering a clinical placement, the following basic points need careful exploration:

- Is it clear exactly what stage the trainee is at with regard to training and what his/her needs are from a clinical placement?
- Are the supervisor and the agency in which the supervisor works really in a position to offer such a placement?
- Can such placements meet the diversity and range of client situations that trainees and courses demand of such placements?
- What, if any, are the links between the placement/supervisor and the training institute in which the trainee is undergoing the training in family therapy?

The clinical placement

The following format is provided to help the training institute, the student and the supervisor develop appropriate and effective clinical placements.

1. The training institute

A growing number of institutions are now providing a full training in family therapy, the formalisation of which has stipulated the number of clinical hours which students must complete in order to progress from one year to the next. With this in mind, the following questions need careful consideration:

a)   To what extent does the training institute assume any responsibility for securing clinical placements on behalf of its students? This is particularly important for students undertaking introductory and intermediate courses. Those encouraging or relying on external supervisors and clinical placements, may wish to consider the value of three-way meetings with the trainee and supervisor at the beginning, middle and end of the placement.

b)   Does the training institute provide an introductory information pack for students seeking placements? This pack should include information about the course the student is studying and the requirements for clinical placements. This information could be given to prospective supervisors by way of introduction.

c)   Does the training institute provide references on behalf of its students?

d)   Does the training institute make it clear what evaluation, if any, is required and what form this might take? This is particularly important given the fact that different courses have different requirements and that students, depending on the level which they have reached during their training, will also have differing needs.

Prospective supervisors might be well advised not to consider students coming from courses where the training institute has not thought fully about its training obligations and has not fulfilled at least some of the requirements mentioned above.

2. The trainee

In approaching a supervisor or agency with a view to securing a clinical placement in family therapy, is the trainee clear about the following points?

a)   The requisite number of hours that he/she must complete within the clinical setting in order to fulfil the requirements of the course. (Trainees must clarify whether additional hours worked in their home base or other external clinical settings count towards their overall clinical hours.)

b)   What form and with what client group he/she must undertake the clinical hours, e.g. observation or direct clinical practice.

c)   What is required of the supervisor in terms of standard, the frequency and the form of supervision, e.g. case discussion, video/audio tape review or live supervision. If the training institute requires the trainee to bring taped sessions of their work from their clinical setting, this must be agreed with the supervisor.

d)   The nature and content of the evaluation in order to successfully complete a clinical placement.

3. The supervisor

Given the increased needs for supervisors, it is not at all surprising that attention has now shifted in the direction of training institutes developing courses with the sole aim of qualifying training supervisors to undertake supervised practice.

In undertaking supervision of trainee family therapists, supervisors are encouraged to consider the following points:

a)   Is the supervisor qualified and in a position to offer such a placement?

b) Has the supervisor devised an introductory pack outlining his/her qualifications, experience, theoretical perspective and the value of his/her agency placement?

c) Is the supervisor's agency in agreement with such a placement and does the supervisor have the support of his/her colleagues?

d) Is the supervisor clear about the agency's requirements for accepting trainee family therapists, i.e. the procedure regarding interviews, taking up references, ensuring medical and police procedures where necessary, the drafting of honorary contracts, etc.?

e) Is the issue of clinical accountability clear?

f) Is the supervisor clear about what is expected of him/her, and is he/she in a position to meet the trainee's requirements?

g) Are the requirements regarding evaluation clear, acceptable and properly incorporated in a signed contract?

h) Has the supervisor devised an induction programme that will helpfully introduce the trainee to the agency, e.g. hours of work, procedures regarding letters to clients, the trainee's title, relationship with other colleagues, outside agencies, the agency's equal opportunities policy, and how the supervisor will incorporate gender, ethnicity, sexuality, etc. into the placement?

i) Has the supervisor organised adequate administration support, access to a telephone, desk, etc.?

j) Would the supervisor value a three-way meeting with the trainee and his/her tutor/group leader from the training institute at the beginning, middle and end of the placement?

k) Is the supervisor clear about who to contact in the event of a difficulty, including the need to terminate the placement?

4. The agency

The following questions need consideration:

a) Does the agency have a document outlining its policies and procedure for new members of staff, i.e. rules of confidentiality, dress code, liability arrangements, professional indemnity insurance, etc.?

b) Does the agency charge for the provision of clinical placements?

c) Does the agency value and encourage clinical placements and have a culture of positively wanting them to work well for all concerned?

Conclusion

The above should not be treated as an exhaustive list, but should be regarded as an attempt to outline possible requirements for training institutions, trainee family therapists and supervisors and their agencies in agreeing the provision of clinical placements.

Tensions may exist in relation to accommodating different supervisory styles within an agreed framework and of squaring the need for assessment and evaluation within post-modern approaches.

The question of vetting and monitoring clinical placements and supervisors is a further level of development awaiting attention.

Finally, it is hoped that the field of family therapy will, in time, respond positively to establishing paid training family therapy posts within agency settings.

Damian McCann and Margaret Bennett
July 1998

Subject Index

Author Index